Create Your OWN WEALTH

DISCOVER THE WORLD OF INVESTMENTS
AND LEARN HOW TO WIN IN THE
STOCK EXCHANGE

ALEJANDRO CARDONA

Create Your Own Wealth

Discover the World of Investments and Learn
How to Win in the Stock Exchange

ISBN-13: 978-0-9974199-2-4

Library of Congress Control Number: 9780997419900

Todos los derechos reservados © 2016 por Alejandro Cardona

Printed in The United States of America
© by Alejandro Cardona

Spanish Editor: A Grace Group, Corp
Translated by: Carlos Mejia
Edited by: Mary Ann Mahoney
Interior Design: A Grace Group, Corp
Cover Design: Juan Salgado

Published by UOPTIONS
Web: www.uoptions.co / www.uopciones.com
Phone: 786 2619 541
Miami, Fl. USA

—

DEDICATION

I dedicate this book to God for saving my life,
to my wife and children for believing in me and joining me
in this beautiful journey.
I thank my parents for giving me the best of them
and for the opportunity to study at the academy.

"The best investment is to learn to invest"
Alejandro Cardona

ACKNOWLEDGMENTS

I thank the following entities
for assisting in the writing of this book:
Marketwatch.com, www.freestockcharts.com, finviz.com
yahoo/finance.com, CBOE, optionslam.com,
www.scottrade.com.

Thanks to their pages and platforms, I was able to share my
techniques and facilitate this knowledge to the world.

INTRODUCTION

Without a doubt for me, the world of stock investments is the most exciting industry in which I have had the opportunity to educate myself in, investigate, experiment, gain, grow, enjoy and now that I want to share with you.

For you to be able to understand my passion and the contagious nature of it; observe a primary group of companies that grew without money such as Apple, Facebook, Twitter, among others, which began as a simple idea, a product or a service and I repeat: they had no money to began with, and started as mere "garage companies"[1]

A secondary group of successful companies exist that acquire earnings with other people's money. There are the investors, investment and retirement funds, in which common people make contributions and invest their money in hopes of achieving through these companies a return of their money and as they say, "save for old age..."

What is the purpose of this investment game? It's simple: **buy low and sell high**. It also works in reverse: they can **sell high and buy low**; this "double opportunity" can only be experienced in the stock market. It is a wonderful thing! Anyone can make money in both booms (where the economy grows) or in recession (where the economy falls).

---

1   Companies that formed out the very basics in a small space.

In this "game of chance" there are upward trends: where it's smart to buy and downward trends where it's smart to sell. For you to understand better, in this book I'll take you through step by step.

Keep in mind that companies need the securities market to move to the next level. It is in the stock market where they find the capital necessary to grow as a business, reach new markets and expand facilities; something that without money, no one could ever achieve. While investors have expectations that their business will grow in the future and therefore, the value of its shares will increase over time.

My great purpose in writing this book is **to give you concrete and very specific tools for a simple and practical way to begin your success** in the stock market. For you to also understand the management of these tools that only a privileged minority use almost in secret, to earn a lot of money.

Are you ready? Prepare yourself, I will take you from the very basics to the most complex so that you may begin your path to economic progress; which is not easy, but is worth knowing. Once you have learned the way, I assure you, you will differ from 90% of the people. You will no longer prefer, like them, to hand your money over to others to obtain average gains without you becoming aware of what is really happening in the financial world.

1

THE MARKET

1. What is the stock market?

Some authors say that the market is the sum of the fear and greed of its participants. Others say that the market is what allows bidders (people who sell) and buyers to find each other, and through organized and regulated systems online, buy and sell financial assets (bonds, stocks, ETFs, commodities, financial derivatives, currencies, etc.).

For me, the market is the most secure way to buy, since the prices are fair at the moment of purchase.[2] This is different from, say, buying a car because there can be a million different prices, at the same time, for the same vehicle.

The market is a gold mine; **you just have to know when to enter the mine and when to leave.**

Furthermore, the stock market has its participants: investment funds, insurance companies, public and private funds, governments, banks, speculators, corporations and individuals, among others. I'd like to clarify again that the purpose of these participants is to make more money and protect their investments against different risks. Companies that are listed in the stock market are public because anyone can be their partner.

2. How can you become a partner of a company?

Buying stock! When you buy stock, you are buying a small part of said company, which allows you to have rights and receive dividends, which depend on the market itself.

---

2 This is the price at which any person could buy at that specific moment.

The other participants of the market are the brokers. Some of the best known are E*Trade, and TD Ameritrade, among others. They are important because through them, you can buy shares, stocks, bonds, exchanged-traded funds (ETFs), currencies and financial derivatives. It is through these authorized institutions that you can buy and sell financial assets. I suggest opening an account in one of these entities; preferably one that has a permanent correspondent in your country. You only need to fill out your name, ID number, address, and other personal information. Verify that it is in fact a commissioned and authorized firm in the stock market.

If you open an account in the United States, for your own security, confirm that the financial entity is endorsed by the U.S. Securities and Exchange Commission (SEC), which can have online access to your account, and do not forget to confirm what the interest rate is for each activity. Additionally, make sure that the platform is user friendly.[3] The majority of these institutions allow, through their respective platforms, a closer look at the history of the graphs and the price of the different actions, as well as having some aids to help you make more informed decisions.

With this information, you will be ready to buy shares online at market price through a broker. We can also make profits on upward and downward trends, a topic that I will expand on later. When we buy a stock, we become partners of that company and we can enjoy dividends. In addition, we are participating in the market alongside professionals who are the 5% minority of the population, yet they take 95% of profits. That is to say, that 5% of participants walk away with 95% of the winnings.

---

3 Operationally, simple to handle.

3. Advantages

These are the aspects that make the stock market interesting, and the advantages that it offers place it above any other commercial activity or service:

1. You can buy and sell stocks, bonds, gold, silver, oil, raw materials (commodities), indexes that track the performance of any sector through ETFs, even the state of the market itself (S&P 500, Dow Jones, Nasdaq, Russell 2000), currencies etc. Don't forget that this is an electronic market, and everything you do goes through a broker and its web platform. Be extra cautious if someone wants to sell you paper shares or bonds. Immediately call the local police and report them.

2. Remember that this is the market that a few that call themselves "millionaires" enjoy. The rich buy shares and assets that tend to gain value over time, while the poor and the middle-class shop in neighborhood stores and supermarkets.

3. You can buy and sell from any location. All you need to conduct business is your account and a computer with internet access. Most people travel long distances to get to work in order to earn $7 dollars3 per hour; which in reality, isn't $7 because they have taken out taxes, contributions, food, car upkeep, tolls and gas.

4. In the stock market, you can achieve elevated or greater profits than any other activity or profession. Later in the book, I'll tell you how to achieve infinite returns with investments and other strategies, in addition, how to generate profits in an upward market as well as downward– something that requires your full attention.

5. For now, I want you to understand something clearly and that is that traditional businesses will grow only when general consumption and the economy are high, and overall credit and production are on the rise. For this reason, I can say that almost every sector struggles during a crisis, while you can make yourself a true millionaire if you choose the correct investment at the correct moment. An example of this were the crises that took place in 2000 and 2008.

In my own judgement, it is in the financial market where the largest amounts of money in the world see movement. Thousands of millions of dollars in transactions take place daily. This is very important because, technically, there are no limitations on capital. This is a world where giants who, with one single order, can increase a stock to 5% or 10% in one day, or in a manner of hours. If you want to buy a stock, it only takes as long as it takes for you to place the order, select the stock and press the "buy" button.

If you want to sell, you simply press "sell". It is that fast and easy. There are thousands of buyers and sellers in addition to the market founders and financial funds that are ready to buy your stock or sell it in the same way. Without a doubt, I assure you that it is the most liquid market I have ever seen and one that you are beginning to enter with this very book.

Normally, when someone buys a business and later wants to sell it, it is no easy task. Similarly, if you buy a property and want to sell it, you will have to wait between two months and even years to be able to make the sale. Something very different occurs in the stock market, where you can enter and exit anytime whenever you want. For example, you can buy a stock of Apple Inc. (AAPL) today and sell it with profit today or tomorrow.

You can also hold onto it for a long period and it will always be there with you, unless the company goes bankrupt or for certain circumstances, it pulls out of the market.

6. Your account is like a business but without fixed costs. That is to say, you do not have to pay monthly bills, employees, rent or public utilities as well as other expenses and obligations that a traditional business takes on. All you need is a computer and internet connection and you can work from your office, which can be Starbucks or an elevator or in line to get into a movie.

7. It is important to know that you can utilize free information found on the internet. Some of the pages that I find most useful are: **marketwatch.com, freestockcharts.com, finviz. com, finance.yahoo.com.** I will explain them later in more detail and how you can use them as they are of great use, and I repeat, they are free!

8. **You can limit your losses.** This means that each time you buy a stock, you can utilize **"stop loss"** which allows you not to risk the entire value of the purchase. On the contrary, through your broker, you can put a maximum limit of risk for your investment in the trading platform.

For example, if you buy Chipotle Mexican Grill (CMG) at $590, you can set the value at which, if the plan does not go well, you can exit. Let's explain "stop loss" with an example. Let's say that the stock fell $15 and you had a stop loss of $15. In other words, if the stock reaches $575 the broker will sell your stock, automatically limiting your losses.

People who faced great losses resulting in financial ruin, depression and even suicide made two mistakes:

- They put more money than they could afford to lose in their accounts
- They never instituted a stop loss

9. I have mentioned some of the advantages that exist in this business but there is one that definitely that takes all the awards, and that is leverage. On your platform, you can apply a "margin" which allows you to buy two, three, four or up to 10 times its capital. This means that you can open your account with $500, but you can operate up to $5,000 with some brokers and platforms. This way, you are using other people's money (OPM) in a manner that is free, because interest rates are very low and you have access to them with these sums.

It doesn't matter if your credit is a disaster, because the money they lend you for these transactions is backed with money you opened your account with, and in most cases that is the maximum loss limit.

Let's take a look at the following example so that you may understand better.

Suppose you open an account with $500 on February 2012 when SPRINT stock was $2.12 per share. With $500, you could buy approximately 230 shares. But let's assume that you had access to a 4/1 leverage, that is to say, you had a buying power of $2,000. With those $2,000, you bought 920 shares and you kept them for 2 years, and in 2014 this stock reached a value of $11. Suppose you sold at that price. The total of the sale would be $10,120 minus the total purchase and sale commissions of $14, minus the time spent that the money was in use, for which in this exercise it would be $50, minus $1,500 that they lent you, and minus my initial capital, the complete operation would look like this:

Earnings: 920 x $11;	$10,120
Minus commissions:	$ 14
Minus the cost:	$ 50
Minus loaned money:	$ 1,500
Minus initial capital:	$ 500
Profits from the operation:	$8,056 U.S. dollars

In other words, you made $8,056 with $500 in two years, which would not have been possible if there were no financial leverage.

At the end of this book, I will share how to use leveraging even up to 100 times with low capital investments.

2

INVESTING WITH SOUND JUDGEMENT

Now that I have told you some of the advantages, we will go deeper into the subject. I will use simple methodologies that will allow you to invest judiciously and not because you heard something on the news, or because someone believes that a stock will go up and down.

Before this, I must mention a few terms used in finance, since learning about finances is like learning a new language.

First, we will use two types of analysis: **Technical analysis** and **fundamental analysis.** Technical analysis refers to understanding the graphs which show what the price history and volume[4] is at any given time. Thanks to the graphs, we can determine whether to buy or sell, and if what we're buying is expensive or cheap. We can see the entire history of the stock as well as different indicators designed to confirm if what you are doing is correct or not. This type of analysis allows you to determine the level of risk, which means setting your "stop loss" or loss limit. It also allows you to decide when to take your earnings or sell your investment. We'll call this **take profit.** For technical analysis, we will work with the website: **freestockcharts.com.**

The fundamental analysis is divided into "macro" and "micro". It is macro where you see the general world economy, or a country's economy. This is done by specifically studying variables like internal consumption, exports and imports, public and private investments, inflation, gross domestic production, a country's rules (which must be optimal for the growth of output), and employment.

The fundamental analysis is micro when you study the specific numbers of a particular company. For example, in the Tesla

---

4   Volume: number of shares purchased and sold over time

Motors (TSLA) report, you can see profitability indicators, sales costs, number of employees, position in the market, if it's a leader or a follower, commercial strategies, etc. For the fundamental analysis, we will use the pages: **finviz.com** and **yahoo.finance.com.**

In the website **marketwatch.com**, we can see the different markets and the hours of operation. It also tells us when the company reports profits and other important news. I anticipate that even with only their "earnings" announcements, you could earn great sums of money. I will explain this in detail further into the book.

Source: Marketwatch.com

The three main global markets that I have mentioned are: **New York,** which is the main one, **London,** and **Tokyo.** In this book, we will center ourselves around the New York Exchange, where the largest companies in the world are listed, as it is still the world's economic main driving economic force. The operating hours are from 9:30 a.m. to 4:00 p.m. EST.

As you can see in the image above, right below New York, it says, 'After'[5], that is to say, hours in which operations are made after the market closes. In the same manner, there exists the 'Pre-Market'. These are actions taken before 9:30 am, and the time

---

5   Operations that happen after the market closes.

factor is decisive in stock market operations. Regarding time, you should be aware that if you do not buy or sell during the established schedule and you turn on your computer after 4:00 p.m. EST, the result can be detrimental to your pocket.

The New York Stock Exchange is the global reference, but that does not mean that NYSE, London Stock Exchange and Tokyo Stock Exchange are the only ones; they are simply the main ones. Countries like Brazil, Mexico, Peru, and Colombia have their stock exchange and stock market, but they are strongly correlated with that of New York. The same goes for the London Stock Exchange, as it serves as the main reference for the entire European market, and Tokyo Stock Exchange for Asia.

To begin to understand the market, we must observe its main indicators. These are so important that from now on, when I mention "the market", I will be referring to these indicators:

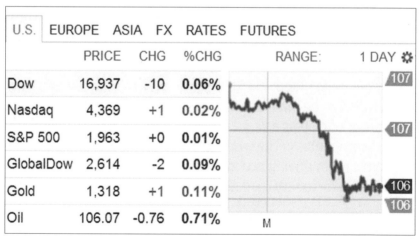

U.S.	EUROPE ASIA FX RATES FUTURES				
	PRICE	CHG	%CHG	RANGE:	1 DAY ☼
Dow	16,937	-10	0.06%		
Nasdaq	4,369	+1	0.02%		
S&P 500	1,963	+0	0.01%		
GlobalDow	2,614	-2	0.09%		
Gold	1,318	+1	0.11%		
Oil	106.07	-0.76	0.71%		

Source: finviz.com

Dow Jones is a weighted average of prices of a bundle of 30 shares, which are the largest currently listed on the New York Stock Exchange. Some of them are:

COMPANIES IN THE DOW JONES INDEX

No.	Ticker	Company	Sector	Industry	Cou
1	XOM	Exxon Mobil Corporation	Basic Materials	Major Integrated Oil & Gas	USA
2	MSFT	Microsoft Corporation	Technology	Business Software & Services	USA
3	JNJ	Johnson & Johnson	Healthcare	Drug Manufacturers - Major	USA
4	GE	General Electric Company	Industrial Goods	Diversified Machinery	USA
5	CVX	Chevron Corporation	Basic Materials	Major Integrated Oil & Gas	USA
6	WMT	Wal-Mart Stores Inc.	Services	Discount, Variety Stores	USA
7	JPM	JPMorgan Chase & Co.	Financial	Money Center Banks	USA
8	PG	Procter & Gamble Co.	Consumer Goods	Personal Products	USA
9	VZ	Verizon Communications Inc.	Technology	Telecom Services - Domestic	USA
10	PFE	Pfizer Inc.	Healthcare	Drug Manufacturers - Major	USA
11	IBM	International Business Machines Corp	Technology	Information Technology Services	USA
12	T	AT&T, Inc.	Technology	Telecom Services - Domestic	USA
13	KO	The Coca-Cola Company	Consumer Goods	Beverages - Soft Drinks	USA
14	MRK	Merck & Co. Inc.	Healthcare	Drug Manufacturers - Major	USA
15	INTC	Intel Corporation	Technology	Semiconductor - Broad Line	USA
16	DIS	Walt Disney Co.	Services	Entertainment - Diversified	USA
17	V	Visa, Inc.	Financial	Credit Services	USA
18	CSCO	Cisco Systems, Inc.	Technology	Networking & Communication Devices	USA
19	HD	The Home Depot, Inc.	Services	Home Improvement Stores	USA
20	UTX	United Technologies Corp.	Industrial Goods	Aerospace/Defense Products & Services	USA

Source: finviz.com

The **Dow Jones** is an indicator that allows us to see if the market is on a downward or upward trend. For example, if we see that the Dow Jones is up 1%, the weighted average of the 30 companies that comprise the Dow Jones has also gone up by 1% that day. This indicator, as well as the **S&P 500**, allows us to see the price history of the U.S. stock market, specifically the market value or equity.

GRAPH 1 | DIA (DOW JONES ETF)

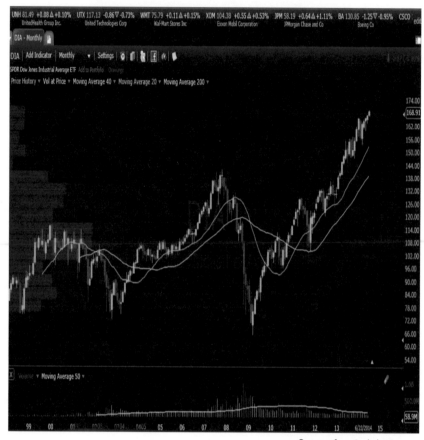

Source: freestockcharts.com

The Dow Jones ETF **DIA** is an **ETF** that follows or is correlated with the Dow Jones. In other words, it has the same behavior graphically to its index.

In **GRAPH 1**, you can see marked the U.S. housing crisis of 2008, and the boom of 2009 to date. In early 2009, the value of the ETF was $66 and now it currently sits at $168.81. That's 256% in approximately 5 years.

Something important to remember is that if you want to buy an index or a commodity (raw material), you need to buy an ETF. It is the same as buying a single stock, it is just named differently, because for something to be a stock it must have a business behind it to back it up. For example, Apple's shares are called AAPL, but if you want to follow the Dow Jones you buy DIA, or GLD if you want to follow gold, etc.

One of the wisest principles I've learned in this process is that the trend is my friend, and I go with it, not against it.

In the case of **GRAPH 1**, the investor who achieved this profit with the Dow Jones in 2009 bought at the time when everyone else was leaving or selling. He instead went along with the trend, earning more money as prices went up for those assets.

We must also remember that the market direction is determined or moved by the big players; giant investors who buy according to their expectations of the economy. In this case, we can conclude that since 2009, the Dow Jones indicator has risen by 2.56 times in value by 2014, that is to say, it has almost tripled.

Another indicator that is of vital importance is the S&P 500 ETF, SPY. Its behavior is show in **GRAPH 2**.

GRAPH 2 | SPY

Source: freestockcharts.com

GRAPH 2 is vital because it allows us to see the history of that asset, as well as telling us if it is at an optimal level to buy or to sell. As you can conclude by looking at the graph, we are in an upward trend. But if we look at the history, we are at the most expensive prices that the stock market has had. Since all financial markets never rise eternally (they have cycles, rises and falls), for now, we will discuss the upward trend.[6]

Another important principle is that history repeats itself and if we don't learn from it, we're doomed to repeat it. And we see that in **GRAPH 2**, where it peaked at its maximum[7] in 2000, and in 2008, when it reached the same level, prices plummeted. The same thing occurred in 2003, when it reached minimum price levels, and in 2009, close to those same levels, it began to rise again. All this is show in the following:

---

6 Upward trend: occurs when prices go upwards, reaching higher prices than previous ones.

7 Maximum: highest price levels in the history.

GRAPH 3

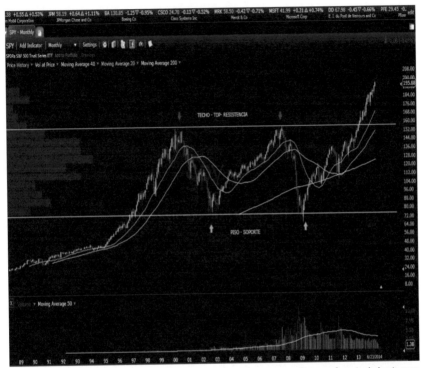

Source: freestockcharts.com

The floor, as we can see in the graph, indicates zones to buy and the ceiling zones to sell. In 2013, the prices exceeded the ceiling, which was then no longer a ceiling but a new reference for the floor.

So far, you should keep in mind that there is a history, one that is evident and repeats itself. The charts do not lie. Therefore, investments should not be based on the opinions of financial gurus, let alone reporters who have never invested. Decisions should be made with the help of graphs and indicators that will help us achieve superior returns with limited risk.

Personally, I believe— and verified for my own safety in many occasions— that the most sensible way to predict the future is through graphs. Graphs help us know at what moment and where we find ourselves in the market. It is very important to know that the "big picture", when it comes to the market, is to know if we find ourselves in a cheap or expensive zone.

Another way to view the market as a whole is to understand and visualize who is involved in it. In this case, the S&P 500 represents the average of the top 500 companies, which may also be registered in the NYSE or Nasdaq, which are the biggest drivers of the market (Market Cap) listed on the American market, as seen in **MAP 1**.

MAP 1

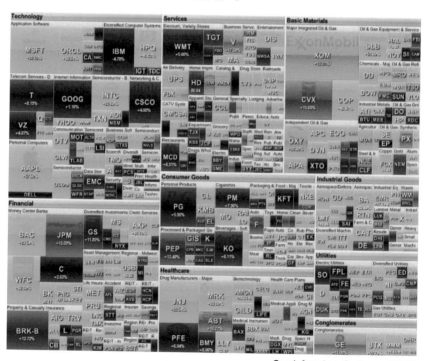

Graph found on: finviz.com MAPS

In **MAP 1**, we can see the biggest companies of the American economy classified by sectors and sub-sectors. It is color coded to help us understand the stocks. Green means growth in prices or 'ups', and downward trends or 'losses' are in red. As we can see on this map, the behavior of the prices that these companies have had (for example, the whole year between June 2013 and July 2014), on average, presented a 25% growth or more.

We can also see that the economy is segmented by sectors, in this case: services, technology, basic materials, financial, consumer goods, healthcare, industrial goods, and utilities.

In yellow, we can the sub-sectors. For this case, I will use the financial sector as an example, and the sub-sectors are: money center banks, credit services, property & casualty insurance, asset management, investment brokerage, credit, mortgage, and administration funds. We then have key sectors, and in addition, subsections that specifically describe the function of each company.

The size of each frame in **MAP 1** is the one that encases and represents each company. The "Market Cap"[8] of each company is what determines the size of the company (size of the square in **MAP 1**). In this order, we can see that Microsoft is bigger than IBM and HPQ, in the same way that AAPL is several times larger than DELL. We can figure out the size of a company by the value of its **Market Cap**. This is how we see that some companies are bigger than others. The fact that one stock is lower in price than another one does not mean anything. The way to compare the size of a company to another is by using the map, specifically through the market cap.

---

8   The number of shares in circulation multiplied by the price at the moment or spot price.

Another important indicator is the **National Association of Securities Dealers Automated Quotation (Nasdaq)**. It is the largest automated electronic stock exchange in the U.S., with more than 3,800 companies and corporations. Out of all the stock exchanges in the world, it is the one that has the most trading volume per hour and has "listed" more than 7,000 shares of small, medium, and large capitalizations. It is characterized by grouping the high-tech companies in electronics, IT, telecommunications, biotechnology, and many others.

Through these two ETFs (NDX & QQQ) we see a summary of the history of Nasdaq's behavior:

GRAPH 4 | NDX-X

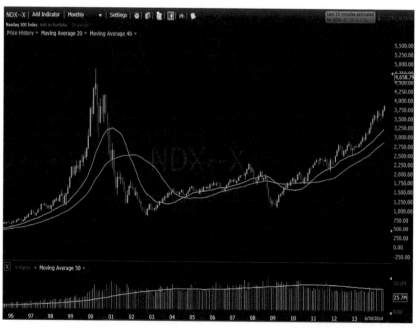

Source: freestockcharts.com

As we can see in the graph, someone who bought this ETF correlated with the Nasdaq in 2009 could obtain it at a price close to $1,000. But in June 2014, it reached a cost of $3,800, which means a profit of $2,800 per ETF in 5 years. That is to say, if someone invested $100,000 on this asset in 2009, in June 2014 they earned $380,000 without using leverage (OPM).

GRAPH 5 | QQQ

Source: freestockcharts.com

In my case, I prefer to operate[9] Nasdaq's ETF (QQQ) in **GRAPH 5**, since it has the same behavior at a more affordable price which makes it easier to buy. Which is better to buy? Something that is worth $92 or something worth $3,800 per unit?

---

9   To perform operations of buying and selling.

This third indicator, Nasdaq, also shows us that we are in an upward trending market, but it is not necessarily thwe most optimal time to buy.

We have learned that the 3 most important market indicators are **S&P 500, NASDAQ, DOW JONES** and their history over time. We understand the long-term trend of each indicator, and some of the opportunities that each offer us to increase our wealth using the market trend as such.

This further demonstrates how money can work for you and much harder in my opinion. Since 2009 to date, new millionaires have been created in the stock market because of these three indicators, and their ability to understand the trends.

Something important to mention is that from this point on, I will refer to the following by their ETFs: S&P 500 as SPY, Dow Jones as DIA, and Nasdaq as QQQ. They are ETFs that have a very important volume, and they allow us to invest to obtain profits, using market trends in our favor.

3

FUNDAMENTAL ANALYSIS

Thehe fundamental analysis found in academic books is complex. For this reason, we intend to convert the complex into something simple, and applicable for you. **When we speak of micro fundamental, we refer to the numbers within a company.** We will use the case of Bank of America.

We can use several indicators to perform a fundamental analysis, however for practical purposes, we will only study a few which have helped me make investment decisions and have been very useful.

On the page **finviz.com**, where it says "search ticker", put the symbol or mnemonic of the stock. For example, Bank of America is abbreviated by the symbol BAC[10], and Apple is abbreviated by AAPL, that is to say, that each stock has their own initials. In this case, we will type BAC and on top of the page, there will be the graph which we won't use for now, and at the bottom there will be the indicators and information that we will analyze.

CHART 1

										financial highlights	state
Index	S&P 500	P/E	20.85	EPS (ttm)	0.75	Insider Own	0.03%	Shs Outstand	10.52B	Perf Week	2.42%
Market Cap	164.46B	Forward P/E	10.31	EPS next Y	1.52	Insider Trans	25.60%	Shs Float	10.50B	Perf Month	6.39%
Income	8.46B	PEG	2.32	EPS next Q	0.31	Inst Own	61.00%	Short Float	0.89%	Perf Quarter	-9.91%
Sales	53.85B	P/S	3.05	EPS this Y	260.00%	Inst Trans	-0.64%	Short Ratio	1.11	Perf Half Y	-0.57%
Book/sh	20.69	P/B	0.76	EPS next Y	65.25%	ROA	0.40%	Target Price	17.19	Perf Year	23.54%
Cash/sh	59.05	P/C	0.26	EPS next 5Y	9.00%	ROE	3.90%	52W Range	12.10 - 18.02	Perf YTD	0.58%
Dividend	0.04	P/FCF	1.90	EPS past 5Y	10.80%	ROI	7.20%	52W High	-13.21%	Beta	1.68
Dividend %	0.26%	Quick Ratio	-	Sales past 5Y	-8.50%	Gross Margin	-	52W Low	29.25%	ATR	0.25
Employees	239000	Current Ratio	-	Sales Q/Q	-8.30%	Oper. Margin	59.10%	RSI (14)	53.46	Volatility	1.61% 1.44%
Optionable	Yes	Debt/Eq	1.17	EPS Q/Q	-150.00%	Profit Margin	15.70%	Rel Volume	0.69	Prev Close	15.45
Shortable	Yes	LT Debt/Eq	1.01	Earnings	Jul 16 BMO	Payout	5.10%	Avg Volume	83.95M	Price	15.64
Recom	2.50	SMA20	1.69%	SMA50	1.91%	SMA200	0.39%	Volume	58,186,480	Change	1.23%

BAC [NYSE]
Bank of America Corporation
Financial | Money Center Banks | USA

Source: finviz.com

---

10 Initials that simplify the name of the company

This is the information that **finviz.com** provides us about the stock of Bank of America. Remember that one stock is a piece of an entire company and is specifically part of the assets in the financial statements. Therefore, if there is no company, there are no stocks. In any case, I mentioned how we will discuss public companies that trade in organized stock markets such as NYSE and NASDAQ. We will filter the information little by little in such a way that you will have the capacity to choose a stock the right way, according to this analysis.

We observe that the first box says **INDEX** and it the case of BAC, this company is a part of the **S&P 500**. Before we continue, I'd like to share another one of my secrets: If you wish to choose a company, it should preferable be part of the S&P 500 or the Dow Jones. I do not recommend investing in "penny stocks" or in companies that do not have a daily average volume of at least 2 million shares.

The box next to it is the Market Cap: in the case of BAC, the value is 164.46 billion dollars. This value is reached by taking the number of shares in circulation **(shs outstand)** located in the fifth indicator column, on the first row, valued at 10.52 billion, and then multiplied by the price of the day, which is $15.54 in this case. Then the value is $164.46 billion.

We also see other variables such as profit **(income)** and total revenue **(sales)**, and it is very important that they have a growing upward trend year after year. We can see these figures in their financial statement format by clicking on the top right corner of the box that reads: **(financial highlights / statements)**. We can also find all this information on **finance.yahoo.com/** by entering the symbol for the company.

It is even more interesting to know that the information is free and available to everyone. We can also find the position of the company we are studying, with the sector as show in **CHART 2**, where the financial figures of the company are compared to that of the sector it belongs to.

**http://www.reuters.com/finance/stocks/
financialHighlights?symbol=BAC**

Let's study the **book/share** or book value. This indicator is important, because it shows us the value of the company's internal accounting, that is, the value of one share according to the actual numbers of the company. In the case of BAC, during the month of June, the book value was $20.69 per share according to its latest report, but the share was trading for $15.64 in the stock market. Therefore, through this analysis, we can say that this stock is on sale or undervalued since values in the stock market trade at a lower price than their real value.

Where does the importance of this indicator come from?

In December 2011, the shares for Bank of America cost $4.92. At the same time, its book/share value was approximately $20, and on March 31st, 2014, BAC was traded at $18. According to this, the market price approached the book value, and the people who bought when it was at $4.92 or close—such as investor Warren Buffett—tripled their fortune in approximately 2 years.

Another case of equal magnitude occurred with Sprint. In 2012, Sprint cost $2.50 per share and in 2014, it was trading at $11. At the moment that the market price was at $2.50, its book/share was at $6 or $7. This indicates to us that the stock was on sale and teaches us a very important lesson:

The rich seek deals in the stock market!

Let's continue with our fundamental analysis of BAC. We can also see the value of dividends per stock,[11] number of employees in the company, and the EPS (the earnings per stock). In the case of BAC, the EPS was $0.75 per stock.

The date assigned to earnings calls is of great importance, and I suggest checking what the earnings report date is before buying any stock because on this very date, there are often abrupt changes in share prices, both upwards and downwards in just one day. In BAC's case, the announcement was made on July 16, BMO, or Before Open Market, which is to say, before 9:30 a.m. that day.

In the following column, we can see profitability indicators. Some of them are:

ROA = Return on assets

ROE = Return on equity

ROI = Return on investments

Something that will set you apart from other investors is understanding that the figures we are analyzing are neither good or bad. We will only know if we compare our company with sector leaders. Making the final click on 'financial highlights', we can find this information:

---

11 Sum of money reported in profit for each share of the company that is in circulation.

CHART 2

MANAGEMENT EFFECTIVENESS

	Company	Industry	Sector
Return on Assets (TTM)	0.45	3.08	3.26
Return on Assets - 5 Yr. Avg.	0.20	2.72	2.88
Return on Investment (TTM)	--	0.00	0.78
Return on Investment - 5 Yr. Avg.	--	0.01	0.76
Return on Equity (TTM)	3.87	24.55	23.07
Return on Equity - 5 Yr. Avg.	0.70	25.51	23.75

Source: http://www.reuters.com/finance/stocks/financialHighlights?symbol=BAC]

Here, we can see that our company, BAC, as far as profitability goes, is below the sector and industry. This is a confirmation that it is not among the most competitive ones. The situation is very different from what is happening in the case of AAPL, whose profitability indicators are above both sector and industry, as shown in **CHART 3.**

CHART 3

MANAGEMENT EFFECTIVENESS

	Company	Industry	Sector
Return on Assets (TTM)	18.82	7.13	13.94
Return on Assets - 5 Yr. Avg.	23.65	8.36	12.30
Return on Investment (TTM)	23.42	11.39	19.17
Return on Investment - 5 Yr. Avg.	30.93	13.77	17.28
Return on Equity (TTM)	29.50	14.63	19.30
Return on Equity - 5 Yr. Avg.	36.56	16.56	16.92

Source: http://www.reuters.com/finance/stocks/financialHighlights?symbol=AAPL

In the report, we can see the EBITDA[12] margins, and compare them to the sector, just as you could do with dividends and levels of debt.

To complete this part, we analyze variable B (Beta) in **CHART 1,** which indicates the correlation of my shares with the market; in this case the S&P 500. We must understand that if the market rises 1%, the variable Beta will tell me approximately how much my shares will rise as well. To figure this out, we must look up "B" found in the last column on **CHART 1.** In BAC's case the B value (Beta) is 1.68, meaning that if the market rises 1%, this stock will rise by approximately 1.68%.

Practically speaking, it is not exact, but it comes close to the value that indicates the average of Beta. This, and other secrets that I will share with you later, is not very well known in the financial world.

---

12 Earnings before taxes, depreciations, and amortizations.

4

ADVANCED FUNDAMENTAL ANALYSIS

I n this chapter, we will study how, through fundamental analysis, we can assess if the company being studied is a market leader. It allows us to see: if the company's key profitability indicators are above or below sector and industry averages, the inherent value of the stock, sales, and income among others. It also helps us to determine whether the stock is overvalued or undervalued, or in other words, if the stock is cheap or expensive according to the financial state of the company. In addition, we can see the history of the main indicators, comparing said financial state, cash flow and balance sheets from different periods for at least the past 3 years.

This information can be obtained on **finance.yahoo.com** or on **finviz.com (financial highlights statements)**.

It is important to know that the value of a company determines its cash flow.[13] But also, we must know that the price we pay to buy a stock of any company is going to be that which the company quotes at that particular moment in the market.

If we see the case of AAPL, the book/share is $19.63 and its spot market price is about $90 approximately. Otherwise, if you want to be a partner with AAPL, you must pay $90 per stock. In other words, no one is going to sell at $19.63, which is what their book value is rather than what their market value is.

---

13 The difference between revenues and cash expenditures indicates if the company is financially viable or not.

CHART 4

Index	S&P 500	P/E	15.19	EPS (ttm)
Market Cap	547.67B	Forward P/E	13.21	EPS next Y
Income	37.71B	PEG	0.99	EPS next Q
Sales	176.04B	P/S	3.11	EPS this Y
Book/sh	19.63	P/B	4.63	EPS next Y
Cash/sh	6.86	P/C	13.24	EPS next 5Y
Dividend	1.88	P/FCF	15.61	EPS past 5Y
Dividend %	2.07%	Quick Ratio	1.60	Sales past 5Y
Employees	80300	Current Ratio	1.60	Sales Q/Q
Optionable	Yes	Debt/Eq	0.14	EPS Q/Q

Source: finviz.com

CHART 4 shows that the P/B ratio has a value of 4.63, and indicates that the stock is overvalued or expensive. If we multiply this value by the book value (19.63 x 4.63), the result is the price of AAPL in the stock market, which is $90.88, which corresponds to the final price of the day on June 23, 2014.

On **google.com/finance, finance.yahoo.com, marketwatch. com,** and **finviz.com**, we will find all the financial information of each company. We can also find who the principle owners are, the board of directors, who the competitors are, the financial state, strategies, and reports that give anyone interested in financial topics a more in-depth financial analysis.

The webpage **finviz.com** also has powerful tools that filter and choose your stocks in the 'screener' section. It gives you the option to choose the country, the volume, which index it belongs to, levels of profitability, dividends percentage, the average volume of the shares, and the range of prices that you are looking for, among other factors.

CHART 5

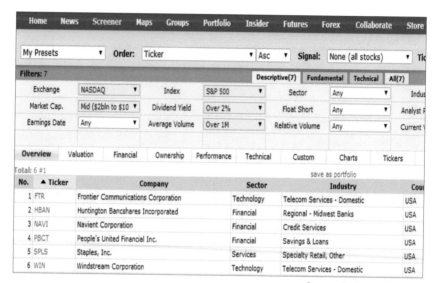

Source: finviz.com/screener

As I mentioned before, I don't invest in companies that are outside the S&P 500. Remember that if you were to buy an ETF like SPY, it would be as if you were buying the average of the 500 biggest companies, which could prove to be a great strategy to you.

In the next chapter. "Technical Analysis," I will show you how to make thousands of dollars with small amounts of money using the three ETF's that I have mentioned (SPY, DIA, QQQ). Through using those three indexes, you will be capable of making more money that you could imagine, not to mention by using very little investment capital.

5

TECHNICAL ANALYSIS

Both **technical and fundamental analyses are important when trying to make educated decisions.** When it comes to technical analysis, we work based on the history, and the history is based on documented events. It is a fact that Netflix (NFLX) reached a price of $53 in late 2012, and is now worth about $440[14] (June 23, 2014). This summarized history of the graphs, which show us where we could find the price of a stock at any given time, is what we will always use to make buying and selling decisions.

It also gives us context as we will know if we are on an upward, downward, or sideways trend. The best website I have found for all this is **freestockcharts.com,** which is an extremely useful and user-friendly tool, which shows data in real-time.

In these types of analyses, you will find an infinite number of indicators, theories, and books; but once you read my secrets, you will receive practical and specific tools that will help you to make correct decisions and make big money.

At the beginning of this book, I told you that the first step is to see the "big picture" of what has happened in the last 15 or 20 years, and in the case of SPY, we can clearly see what has happened and detect the ceilings and floors which were formed during 1990—2014. Furthermore, it shows us that we are on an upward trend. It's like seeing the earth from a satellite; looking at it from afar.

Our next step will be to zoom in closer to the big picture. We will look at the period between 2009 and 2014, since that is the date that the market stopped falling any further (respecting a hard floor or support) and began the upward trend, as shown in **GRAPH 6.**

---

14 Before split

GRAPH 6

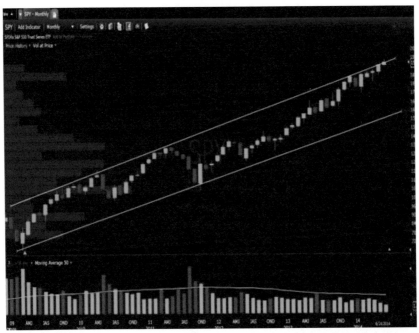

Source: freestockcharts.com

As seen in the graph, SPY (S&P 500's ETF) is clearly in an upward trend. It has a channel-like tendency which I have delineated with white lines, where we can also clearly see the floors and ceilings of the trend. This allows us to conclude, based on the history, that we are upward trend and that during this trend, there are levels where investors buy and others sell. We can see that there are upward and downward movements within this period of time, and this explains why investors should sell to materialize their earnings and turn them into cash when they have made a profit.

Similarly, there are levels in which to buy. This creates new increases in prices until they once again reach the top of the trend, as seen at the end of the graph. All this brings us to the conclusion that we are at high price levels, according to the history, and could have some drops in the coming months unless it breaks the ceiling of the trend and reaches higher price levels.

The next step will be to bring the big picture a bit closer and proceed to check some other concepts such as the Japanese candlesticks, moving averages, and the moving average converge/divergence (MACD) indicator; important terms that will facilitate your comprehension of the market.

Let's take a look at the 'big picture' during the year and a half between 2013 and 2014. This will help us decide whether it is wise to buy now or if we should wait, and also to visualize what has transpired in this time period.

GRAPH 7

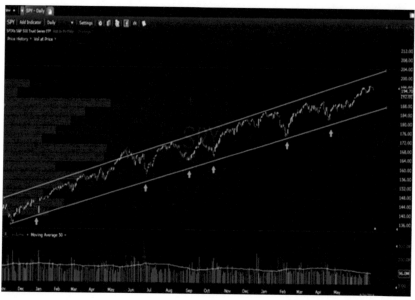

Source: freestockcharts.com

GRAPH 7 shows us what occurred between November 2012 and June 2014. We see an upward trend that allows us to define shorter cycles of days and weeks. I have marked with green arrows the most successful points of purchase. As you can see, the best time to buy is when it is at the lower zones marked by the green arrows, because it is "cheap." On the other hand, the best time to sell is when the prices are approaching the upper line of the channel.

(I want to remind you that the white lines are traced by touching or attempting to touch most of the points on the bottom as well as on top.)

It's important to sell when it touches the top part of the channel, and if you don't, prices may fall until it touches the bottom part. By looking at the graph, we can conclude that this is an upward trend because even though it rises and falls, it only ascends inside the channel.

Those who have bought when the prices have touched the bottom part of the channel, as well as those who have sold when it touched the top, have obtained important earnings. Said purchasing opportunities have presented themselves approximately 7 times in a period of 18 months. With the previous I do not mean to say that this is the only way to make money, but I do think it is the safest way and one that has worked best for me.

By this point, you should have the capacity to understand when it is smart to buy and sell with the most important indicators in the world. In other words, you are now trained to make money!

6

CANDLES

Now, let us get more familiar with some indicators and variables that will facilitate the decision-making process. On the graphs from **freestockcharts. com** that I have shown in this book, you will find rectangular figures with green and red lines. These are called "candlesticks" (**FIGURE 1**) and, as we know, green represents increments in the price in a determined period of time, and red represents a fall in the prices.

The candlesticks are important because they give us signals to buy and sell, but also because they mark four essential prices for us: **maximum, minimum, opening, and closing**. Remember that the market opens at 9:30 a.m. and closes at 4:00 p.m. New York Time. **One candlestick can represent 1 minute, several months, or even years, as you can set it to any unit of time you desire.** Up until now, we have used months and days in all the previous graphs.

If we assume the unit of time is 'monthly', each candlestick is going to represent a different month and their opening price would be the first day of each month at 9:30 a.m. The closing price would then be marked at 4:00 p.m. on the last day of the month. During this month, there was a maximum price and a minimum price but they were not necessarily the opening and closing prices. They were simply the prices at the times the trades took place throughout the month. We can see this in **GRAPH 8.**

FIGURE 1

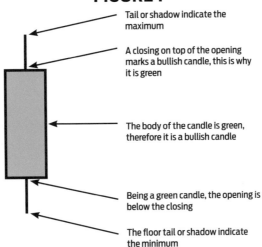

Tail or shadow indicate the maximum

A closing on top of the opening marks a bullish candle, this is why it is green

The body of the candle is green, therefore it is a bullish candle

Being a green candle, the opening is below the closing

The floor tail or shadow indicate the minimum

GRAPH 8

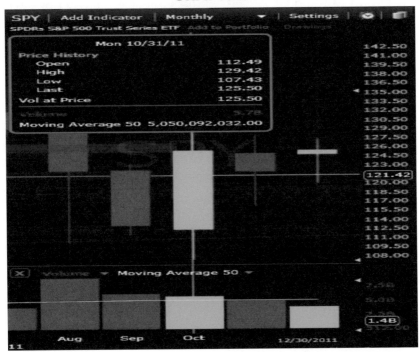

Source: freestockcharts.com

The candlestick being observed is the **big green candle** to the right of the two red candles. This candlestick represents the month of October in 2011. As we can see, the candlestick has two tails, one on top and another one on the bottom. These tails mark the maximum and minimum prices that were traded during that month.

GRAPH 8 shows us the minimum price which was traded at $107.43 and the maximum price which was traded at $129.42.

The first price recorded during the month was the opening price which, in this case, was $112.49 and the closing price was $125.50. With these four prices, you can draw your candlestick for this month. The tails will once again give us the maximum and minimum. If it is a green candle, the opening price will be on the lower part of the body of the candle, while the closing price will be on the top part, as **FIGURE 1** shows.

The red candle represents drops in the price, and the opening will be on the top part of the body and the final or close price will be found on the bottom. Since we are working with Cartesian geometry, the maximums will be at the top while the minimums will be at the bottom. This is something you should remember, some people are often confused when drawing red candles and the only thing that changes between the two candlesticks is the position of the opening and closing price. The red candle would then look like this:

FIGURE 2

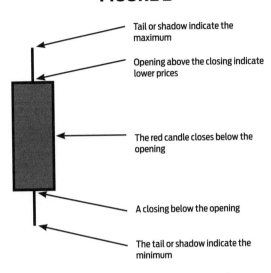

Tail or shadow indicate the maximum

Opening above the closing indicate lower prices

The red candle closes below the opening

A closing below the opening

The tail or shadow indicate the minimum

Now you should understand why graphs are constructed based on these candles and what the four prices are, which are vital when buying or selling.

The candlesticks also indicate signals of when to buy and sell. Later on, we will take a look at the tools that I consider to be the most helpful. What I can say with certainty is that the market is very generous. It tells us when to enter, exit, and when a trend is about to end, and if you know how to read it, you can become a prosperous person.

The market has no limits, and it does not matter where a person finds themselves or how much money they may have. If they learn to understand the market, they can live off of this activity and live quite well. Candlesticks also let you know if we are buying in first or last. As mentioned at the beginning, markets do no rise indefinitely but move in a wave pattern, and even if they are in an ascending direction, they go up and down within that trend.

TESLA CASE

Let's observe what is presented in the candlesticks for the Tesla Motors company:

GRAPH 9

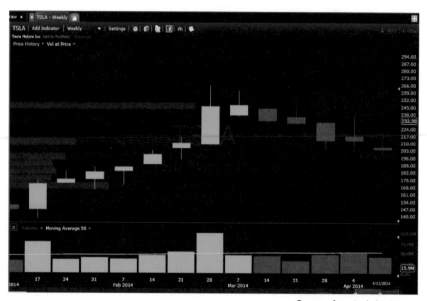

Source: freestockcharts.com

In **GRAPH 9,** we can see the candlesticks representing weeks between the months of January and April of 2014. As you can see in the graph, this company's prices rose for 8 weeks straight, that is to say, that those who bought TSLA on week 8 lost money because they bought last.

Subsequently, during the following five weeks, the stock of TSLA MOTORS had a fall in prices week after week, but as we now know, this was not indefinite either.

ROSS CASE

Let's study a different case, Ross Stores. (ROST):

GRAPH 10

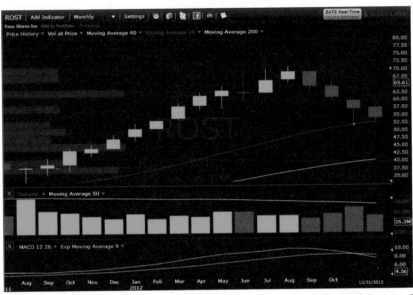

Source: freestockcharts.com]

As show in **GRAPH 10,** ROSS's stock increased for about 13 months. But once again, after a sharp climb, come market corrections because the investors need to liquidate their profits.

Another important factor by which a stock can correct its tendency is through **earning reports**. This topic in particular I will discuss later, and will also explain how to make money with said reports.

Candlesticks are important because they give signs of **buying, selling, and changes** in tendency. Some candlesticks like the **Hammer** and the **big green** candlestick, show us valuable opportunities.

GRAPH 11

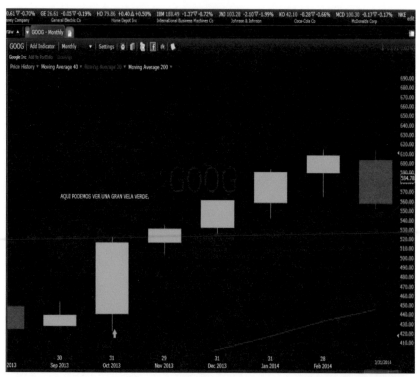

Source: freestockcharts.com

After a candle presents itself with a body almost three times as big the previous one as seen above, it is usually followed by additional price increases. In this case, after the large green candle appeared, the stock rose from about $520 to $610.

The other candle that has given me the best results in my trading experience is the hammer, which indicates entry opportunities to buy in an upward trend.

GRAPH 12

As the graph above shows us, when a "hammer" candlestick appears, it can be recognized by a solid body on top and a tail underneath it. It is telling us, "I will not fall anymore." Here, candlesticks with hammer are marked with green arrows.

The hammer represents a negotiation for the drop in prices, but we must find ourselves in an upward trend within the period of time we are in as seen on the graph for S&P 500. In many occasions once a 'hammer' candlestick appears, while respecting the trend line, it tends to have important increases in prices.

7

THE MOVING AVERAGES

The "moving average" allows us to confirm the current trend; that is, it lets us be sure if we are in an upward or downward trend, as well as help us determine if what we're buying cheap or expensive.

To clarify this, let's take a look at **GRAPH 13.** We know that the candlesticks are the four prices of the day, week, year, hour, or whatever unit of time we determine on the platform. Under the prices, we can see a dark blue line (moving average 20), another one that is yellow (moving average 40), and a white one underneath them (moving average 200). These lines are the price averages of the last 20, 40, and 200 weeks, in this case. Additionally, these averages move alongside the candlesticks as time progresses.

GRAPH 13

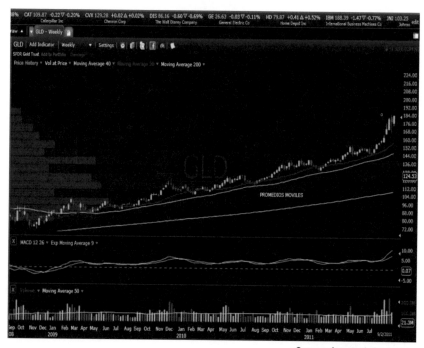

Source: freestockcharts.com

It is very important to know how to construct an indicator as they will be a great tool in achieving your desired profit. On the webpage, **freestockcharts.com,** you only need to click **"add indicator"** (add indicator > moving average > price history), and the line appears automatically. Once the line is drawn in the top part of the graph, you can click on the average and click **"edit"** to change the 50 for 20. You can repeat this exercise 3 times so that in the end, you obtain the 3 moving averages shown in **GRAPH 13**.

Like I mentioned, the averages help us to confirm the trend. In **GRAPH 13,** we see appear an upward trend and we can recognize it because first, the candlesticks or prices are above the lines of the averages 20, 40, and 200. Second, the lines of the averages look like railroad tracks, meaning they are parallel in an ascending direction and continue to go up. Third, to recognize this upward trend, the prices have to be above the moving average of 20, and this one should be above the 40, and lastly be above the 200, as seen in **GRAPH 14**.

A key factor of being successful during a trend like the one on **GRAPH 13** is **to buy closest to the average and sell far from the average**. If the prices are close to the lines inside a trend, it is indicating that we should buy, and when the prices are far from the average, it is telling us to sell, or leave our position.

In **GRAPH 14**, the green arrows point to the buying points, and the red arrows point to selling points.

GRAPH 14

Source: freestockcharts.com

GRAPH 14 allows us to recognize clear upward trends, but we can also visualize the entry points (purchase) and the exit points (sale). As you can see on the last part of right side, Gold (GLD) reached a level of $186. Those who bought at that time were far away from the average and lost due to prices correcting themselves and returning close to the average lines, and price levels close to $162. I want you to understand that this is a big lesson to learn.

That is to say, **you now know when to buy and when to sell stocks using the moving averages.** The majority of people buy based on emotions or because "I heard", "I believe", "I think", and these do not work in the financial world. We must have a strong technical support foundation to make buying and selling decisions. The averages are great allies because they help us detect what is about to occur in the market. It also helps us to know when a downward trend is about to change to an upward one, and vice versa. When the averages cross, or in other words, when they don't look like the parallel lines of a railroad, and they touch and intersect instead, this would indicate a change in trend.

In **GRAPH 15**, we can see the trends and the points at which the averages crossed each other, indicating future changes. Looking at the Google stock, we can see a period where there was an upward trend on the left side of the graph, until the averages started to cross, leading us to a downward trend. This trend is characterized by the prices being below the moving averages.

We can also see in **GRAPH 15** that the blue and yellow lines are above the prices or candlesticks, until they cross again in May 2014, indicating an upward change. If we look at the price changes from May to July 15, 2014, Google reaches prices upward of $500 per share in May, and only a month and a half later, it is at $584 per share. This is an increase of close to 20% in less than two months. This, to some investors, would easily represent millions and hundreds of millions of dollars in profit.

It is advantageous for you to know how to use this information and how to use the correct investment tool.

GRAPH 15

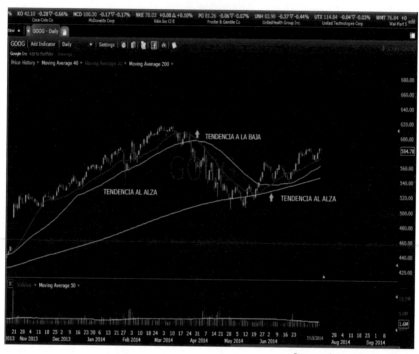

Source: freestockcharts.com

The moving average of 200 is depicted by the white line on the graph. In my experience, this is of great use, because it gives me signals of when to buy. This occurs when the moving average is touched and its level respected. That is to say, when the candlestick touches the white line, or moving average of 200, we see that instead of continuing to fall, the prices start rise, which is a great opportunity to quickly make important profits.

In 2014, we see that GOOG was listed at levels of $520 per share, and if you count the green candlesticks, it went up for 6 days straight until it reached $565 approximately, producing a $45 profit per share in a period of 6 days. This doesn't seem like a big deal, but remember that investors use leverage (making more money with less money), and many times this leverage can multiply your capital up to 100 times. Thus, $45 in reality is $4,500 in profit, and even more when considering each stock. This I will explain later in greater detail.

In **GRAPH 16,** we can better see the entry point to buy with the moving average of 200, where in the lower left, the prices are close to the white line which indicates a buying opportunity.

GRAPH 16

Source: freestockcharts.com

In the same way, the moving averages allow us to operate in any unit of time. We can see units of time in one hour and analyze some opportunities, for example, Chipotle Mexican Grill (CMG):

GRAPH 17

Source: freestockcharts.com

As you can observe in **GRAPH 17,** once the prices touch the moving average of 200 in one hour, they start rebounding and rising in significant prices in short periods of time. The first time it touched the average during the 8th and 9th in July, the stock went from $580 to $608, an increase of 28 points in practically one day. On the second occasion, the movement was barely getting started, but it respected the previous established level and in only one day, it was already up and close to $8 per stock.

CONCLUSION:

We can say that the moving averages help us confirm the trend, its changes, and detect buying and selling opportunities in different financial assets. They are of vital importance and they announce changes that can translate into large sums of money. The moving averages act as ceilings and follow the levels of support and resistance inside a defined trend.

An even more important conclusion is: never buy far from the moving averages because prices move in waves, meaning they rise and fall. The averages also help you recognize how far or near the prices are to the optimal buying and selling locations. (See **GRAPH 15, 16, and 17**).

8

SUPPORT AND RESISTANCE

By reviewing the history of different active prices, we can find that the investors keep track of past prices. That is to say, they remember what happened when a stock reached a certain level of pricing and the reaction it had, which can motivate them to buy or sell.

Let's take a look at several cases during different time frames to help us understand this:

GRAPH 18

Source: freestockcharts.com

In this graph, we can see the prices of CMG from August 12th, 2014, to approximately September 5th. The prices are in units of hours; each candlestick signifies one hour inside the stock market business hours of 9:30 a.m. to 4:00 p.m., United States Eastern Time.

In this graph, I have drawn a horizontal line at the bottom and another one at the top, with the purpose of identifying the levels of buying and selling. A level of buying is identified when the prices don't fall lower than said level two or more times. In this case, we can see that each time the price of this stock touches 674, it begins to go up until the reaches prices between 685 and 693, where the prices begin to fall again.

That behavior can repeat itself for some time, but once it breaks these initial channels—which we will call "floor" and "ceiling" or "support" and "resistance"—, new patterns will usually form in the same manner. Our jobs as investors consist of identifying and taking the highest advantage of these events.

In the following, we can see other cases of Support and Resistance.

In **GRAPH 19**, we can see the stock from Best Buy (BBY). The unit of time that we will use is monthly, meaning that each candlestick represents a different month on the graph.

The reader will now be capable of identifying that the floor (or support) is in the price range between $11 and $12, while the ceiling (or resistance) is located between $42 and $45, all while both levels are respected by not having prices break them. That is to say that when the stock reaches those prices, they have represented buying and selling opportunities.

GRAPH 19

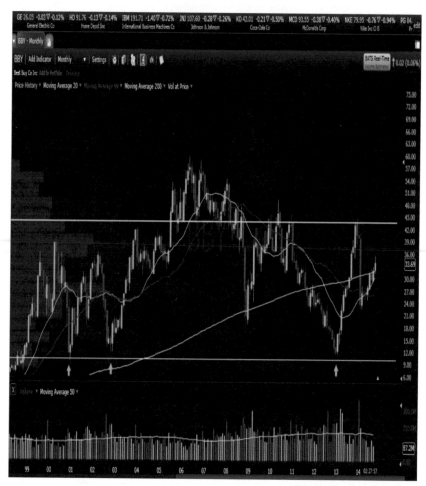

Source: freestockcharts.com

Another important aspect of the support and resistance levels is that they allow us to determine, in a professional way, our levels of risk and potential sale. These are our levels of "Stop Loss" and "Take Profit." The Stop Loss indicates the maximum levels of loss and the Take Profit indicates a specific level of profit when your stock should be sold. Let's observe a practical example:

PRACTICAL EXAMPLE:

Let's assume that Mr. X has $100,000 and saw that Best Buy (BBY) had reached price levels of approximately $11 per stock. When the stock was previously in that price level, between the years 2001 and 2003, he observed that during those years, the stock began to rise. Furthermore, he observed that this could occur once there was a rebound, meaning that the stock would no longer be falling and instead the candlestick would start to turn green. In this manner, Mr. X could intelligently make such investment.

Mr. X observed is that the stock's price had been falling since 2012 for 6 months straight. After he scrolled to the left to observe the history of previous time periods, he noticed that after rebound could be coming (which is an opportunity to make money).

Mr. X did not buy on a red candlestick **(note this in your rules notebook)**. The key is to buy on a green candlestick and sell on a red one. He bought when he saw that the stock began to rise, respecting the support that was outlined in the time period of 2001 and 2003, respectively. In addition, these levels helped him pin down his loss limit or Stop Loss. His financial analysis was the following:

PRICE OF PURCHASE: $12.50 per stock
INVESTMENT CAPITAL: $100,000
NUMBER OF STOCKS TO BUY: 8,000 units

STOP LOSS or MAXIMUM LOSS ALLOWED: $10,000, meaning that $11.25 is the maximum price it should fall. This means that if he had bought 8,000 stocks of BBY, the result would $100,000, but if the price dipped to $11.25, his portfolio would have be worth $90,000; a loss, in this case, of $10,000, which was his value of risk. That did not occur as such since this level was noticed on the graph and was noticed through the history of BBY.

TAKE PROFIT: When Mr. X had made his purchase, he knew that once the stock reached levels of $25, he would sell 50% of his stocks and leave the remaining 50% in case the stock reached $40, which is when he would sell the remainder.

The previous exercise can be summarized like this:

SELL 50%: 4,000 stocks at $25, for a total of $100,000. At this time, Mr. X was able to retrieve his initial investment, and the investment that remains is risk-free, since he has already taken out his initial capital.

He still has 4,000 stocks with an additional total value of $100,000. Mr. X waits until these stocks reach $40, and once they do, he sells the 4,000 stocks for $160,000 which represents his net profit. This took place over the span of 10 months. The profit percentage in this exercise is technically infinite since there was not a value or capital at risk.

As you can see from this example, the support and resistance levels are a practical tool to help us make informed decisions. They help us control our levels of risk and help us identify potential areas to sell

9

STRATEGIES

Before investing, the most important thing is knowing what our level of risk is, as well as the possible level of profit that we could obtain to determine if our strategy is suitable or not. You'll know if you have a winning strategy by analyzing previous graphs to see if the odds are in your favor before making any decisions.

Example:

In **GRAPH 19**, you can see the case of BBY. The risk of each stock was $1.25 and the potential benefit previously was, according to the graph, $40 (levels of roof) – $12 (levels of support or floor during 2001 – 2003) = $28 (potential utility). This strategy can be summarized as follows:

Potential reward: $28 + **Potential risk:** $1.25 = $22. Meaning the strategy would be 22/1. One of risk vs. 22 of reward.

As you can see, in this type of strategy, there are more probabilities in your favor. My experience confirms that one winning strategy must have a greater probability than 4/1.

To calculate the relationship of a winning strategy, we must take the dollars, or whatever unit of potential profit we are working with, and divide them by the risk or a defined stop loss limit. If the relationship is greater than 4, then we can say that it is a good strategy, as long as the graph analysis is correct.

Money Management

A rule of personal investment that one must follow is: place in your investing accounts only what are you willing to risk.

People who suffer financial bankruptcy because of their investments always violate this rule and trade or speculate with mowney that did not belong to them, or with sums that they cannot afford to lose or have designated for other plans.

Now that you know this, it is recommended that you:

1. Never borrow money to perform these types of investments.

2. Do not invest amounts that could affect your mental, emotional, or physical health if its lost.

3. Do not borrow money from your friends or relatives to invest.

Money management also means that we need to be clever and begin by managing small amounts of money, so later we will be able to manage larger sums.

For example, a person who has an account of $500 should not take the $500 and use it all on one stock. On the contrary, they should take a smaller amount such as $50 or $100 to start with, and when these sums show positive results, then you can start to handle a larger one, all while acquiring more experience as an investor.

Another important aspect of money management is to always be defining your limits, for profit as well as for loss and using winning strategies as we have previously seen.

Remember that later in this book, you will read about leverage, i.e., making big money with little money. For this reason, $500 are not in reality that sum but probably 10, 20, or 100 times more.

Another aspect of money management is discipline. A disciplined investor sells once they have met their goal, since they understand that the market rises and falls. If they don't, they may lose their earning as well as their initial capital. Likewise, if the investment does not turn out as expected, the disciplined investor sells and exercises their loss limit, as they understand that is preferable to lose a part of it than to lose it all.

Later, we will talk about money management while handling 'options' specifically, a leverage tool that will enable you to earn more money with little money and with limited risks.

TRENDS:

Remember that one of the most important principles is: **"the trend is my friend and I never go against it."** We can find three types of trends:

1. Upward
2. Downward
3. Lateral

You can find markets in an upward trend, for example, in S&P 500 during the years of 2009 to the first trimester of 2015. Downward trends are also found in SPDR Gold Trust (GLD), iShares Silver Trust (SLV), and the United States Oil Fund (USO). We can also find lateral trends where prices remain in horizontal ranges during a considerable period of time, as in the case of JPMorgan Chase (JPM).

In this book, we are going to study these trends, but we will mainly focus on the upward trend, due to the fact that the market is currently in one and it would be of great use to the users.

Keys to recognizing an upward trend:

1. Prices ascend in real time.
2. Prices, or candlesticks, are above the moving averages 20, 40, 100, and 200 in unit of time "daily".
3. Upward channels form, i.e., prices rise and fall but they do so within a channel where they are always reaching new higher prices.
4. There are cheap zones where it is wisest to buy (the lower part of the upward channel).
5. There are expensive zones where it is wisest to sell (at the top of the upward channel).

GRAPH 20

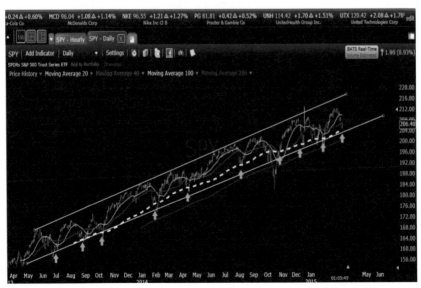

Source: freestockcharts.com

Let's study these by using the S&P 500, which summarizes the history of the American stock market. As we see in **GRAPH 20**, a clear upward channel has formed in the S&P 500, where prices tend to rise when they touch the lower part of the channel, as marked by the green arrows, at which point the most intelligent thing to do is to buy. In the same way, the top of the channel indicates that it is time to sell. If not, profits can be lost as time goes by.

Example:

Analyzing the July 2013 period, we can see that the prices touched the lower part of the channel where it was smart to buy, given that it had low risk according to the history and a higher earning potential than that of the risk. At the time, the spot price was $157 for each SPY ETF. Suppose that we are willing to risk $2 per ETF, and by looking at the area that it could rise up to, we would know that it could reach prices of up to $170. This means that my potential reward was $13 vs a risk of $2. This can be defined as a winning strategy because if we calculate the reward/risk, we get the following result:

Reward $13 + Risk of $2 = 6.5 or 6.5/1

In the previous example, we can see that the probabilities are in your favor, and the proportion of profit is much greater than the risk. It is important to do calculation because prior to investing, we must calculate and be prepared for any eventuality. The plan should be the following: If things go wrong, you lose $2 per ETF and exercise stop loss, meaning that you sell with a small amount of loss. If things go well and the market rises, you will earn approximately $13 per ETF.

Exercise:

Suppose that you bought 1,000 SPY ETFs at a price of $157 each. The total investment value would then be $157,000 + $7 of commission with a total of $157,007. If SPY went down to $155, you would sell, only losing approximately $2,000.

But the reality is that SPY rose to a price of $170 where the sale is made at that price with a total of $170,000 minus commissions that do not even reach $20. Total approximate gain: $13,000 in the period of one month. That is an approximate profit of an 8% nominal monthly rate.

10

PERFECT ENTRY AND MACD

As you have already read, your job is to buy intelligently when the market is on sale. However, it's important to keep in mind additional indicators before making the decision to buy, which I describe in the following five points:

1. In **GRAPH 21,** the trend is clear and prices tend to rebound when they touch the bottom of the channel, which translates to opportunities.

2. An excellent indicator is a "hammer" candlestick with a long tail, which indicates that prices were falling but are quickly starting to rise again. It is important that the candlestick appears at the lower part of the channel. After this occurs, a green candlestick must appear, indicating a rebound, which confirms that the market will continue with the upward trend.

3. With SPY, the moving average that best helps you to clearly identify the rebounds is the moving average of 100. If you take a look at the history, each time the prices reach that level of 100, they tend to bounce back and continue the trend.

4. Another helpful indicator is the MACD, which also confirms whether we are in a zone of purchase or sale. I will mark with green arrows where the MACD signals that a purchase should be made.

5. Finally, it is important to change the unit of time to "hourly" if we are close to the moving average of 100 on the "daily" graph. Then, where are cross between averages takes place, indicating that the prices are not falling anymore and that they are confirming the change in trend. I suggest you take a few minutes to look at **GRAPH 21** to make your own conclusions regarding points 1 to 4. After this, take some time to analyze **GRAPH 22** to make the same conclusions regarding point 5.

We can see in **GRAPH 21** that when prices touch the lower portion or moving average 100, it begins to rise.

GRAPH 21

Source: freestockcharts.com

By using these two cases, we can also identify the hammer candlesticks that precede the rise in prices, and on the bottom of the channel, we can see the crossing of MACD. This confirms that prices are in buying zone, and from then on, it is very likely that prices will keep rising in this stock. Something I'd like to highlight is that history teaches us that these increases last between approximately 3 and 4 weeks, and the ascending movement is between $10 and $15 on average, which gives us the earnings range.

Let's see what should happen in the "hourly" time frame. For this, on the webpage **freestockcharts.com**, we must change the units from "daily" to "hourly". And what should appear in the lower zone is the following:

GRAPH 22

Source: freestockcharts.com

While in an "hourly" time frame, we need to understand that the definitive sign is when the prices change from a downward trend to an upward one when the moving averages of 20 and 40 cross in one hour. From then on, an upward trend will start forming once again, where we can apply the "falls are opportunities" strategy. We must also buy when close to the moving averages and sell when far from them, based on the history, waiting for the rupture of the downward channel in an "hourly" time frame.

An upward trend in the stock markets is a great opportunity to create your own money. It is only a matter of understanding and studying them to get the most economic benefit:

1. You should know when the prices are on sale and sell when we have achieved our profit goal.

2. It is important not to let fear or greed dominate your investment decisions.

3. The buying and selling decisions must be based on real facts, meaning graphs and not emotions or personal opinions.[15]

4. Only when we manage to be objective and diligent will we achieve success in our investments.

---

15 Personal emotions have not contributed to my process as an investor in a positive way. That is my experience and I gladly share it with you and leave it for you to reflect on.

Other important conclusions of the trend:

1. Falls are opportunities, but only if we find ourselves in an upward trend. (See **GRAPH 23**).

2. Cycles repeat themselves and we must be prepared to take action.

3. The smartest thing to do during upward trends are 'long sales', that is, buy cheap to sell expensive. Use CALLS.

4. It is not recommended that you make 'short sales' (PUTS) because sometimes the prices get stuck near the roof of the channel and then continue to rise. This would bring losses to that type of purchase as time went on.

5. The MACD should preferably be in a low area of the channel, below the zero line, and then we wait for the crossing. Study the MACD in a "daily" graph).

6. The hammer candlestick is an indicator that helps you make informed purchasing decisions just as long as it is in the lower part of the channel, and is followed by a green candle in daily and represents a rupture of the channel.

7. If prices exit the trend of the channel, it is prudent to wait and see if they will re-enter the channel, otherwise it would be telling us a change in trend coming up. To understand this point, take a look at SPDR Gold Trust (GLD) in the period of 2012.

GRAPH 23

Source: freestockcharts.com

GRAPH 23 shows us a typical upward trend where prices (green and red candlesticks) on the top part of the candlesticks are above moving averages 20 and 40 (the yellow and green line). In this type of scenario, the falls are buying opportunities, **especially when they touch the moving average 40 (hourly).** Remember that the moving averages also represent the supports or floors from where prices tend to rebound.

As we have seen, in the S&P 500 (SPY), which is in the daily unit of time up until now (first trimester of 2015—"actual date"), the moving average of 100 is the most accurate support. As observed in **GRAPHS 21 and 24**, when prices touch this average, they tend to have a rise of approximately 10 points.

We can also see that while analyzing SPY in hourly, the most important moving averages are usually 20 and 40, especially 40 as seen in **GRAPH 23**. In it, we see increases in very short periods of time, between 2 to 6 points in just a few hours.

In summary, the previous information offers specific data on to generate profits in the biggest stock market in the world.

Additional tools to perform a perfect trade:

At this point, you should know that S&P 500, just like NASDAQ and Dow Jones, tends to respect the moving average of 100, but I was able to prove that this is not always the case. Therefore, we need more accurate data to make purchasing decisions.

I am not saying that the moving average of 100 is not important, because it is, and the graph demonstrates this. But we must take an additional step, and that is to trace downward lines in an hourly time frame. This is useful as it helps us to know exactly where to buy.

You can watch videos where I make money in real time, using the tools that I have shared with you. To view them visit **uoptions.co.**

Using hourly and daily graphs, I will share with you a wonderful strategy that is more likely to win than to lose.

GRAPH 24

Source: freestockcharts.com

This graph shows us what has been occurring in S&P 500 since the end of 2012: each time it touches the white line (moving average of 100), buyers react and make prices rise in a period of less than 30 days.

That is to say, the investors who bought when prices touched this indicator (100) made money quickly. Keep in mind that not everyone may earn the same even if they have bought at the same prices because this depends on how much leverage[16] has been used.

GRAPH 24 shows us that prices rise, fall, and tend to rise again when they touch the floor of the moving average of 100. The second step is to put "hourly" in the time tab when prices begin to fall. At the same time, we will trace a line from the top part. This ceiling is the one that helps us to recognize when prices will stop falling and will begin to rise once again; this is where we must pay close attention as to when to invest, especially in SPY. We must also use a daily graph and prices to be close to the moving average of 100.

GRAPH 25 shows this taking place. Keep in mind that **GRAPHS 24 and 25** are the same, they are simply set in different units of time, "daily" and "hourly".

Since **GRAPH 24** is a daily one, it means that in this strategy, each candle is one day. **GRAPH 25** is an hourly one, telling us that each candle represents one hour (between 9:30 a.m. .and 4 p.m. EST).

---

16 Leverage: to make more money with less personal capital.

GRAPH 25

Source: freestockcharts.com

The green arrow in **GRAPH 25** shows us exactly where to buy. The lines at the top are drawn on **freestockcharts.com.** You must do this on your own; it is something very simple and you should get used to drawing them. Remember that on the website **uoptions.co** we teach you how to do this in an easy, simple, and straightforward way through videos.

In **GRAPH 25,** we can also see the buying and selling points, so we have an idea of the profits for each stock or ETF purchased. All of this looks very interesting, but you would need large sums of money to make even more money.

To better explain this, I will give you the following example:

Suppose that we buy 100 units of SPY at a price of $202 each. For this, we would need an investment of $20,200. Then, 20 days later, we would sell at a price of $211, that is, we would get $21,100 where the total profit without commissions would be $900. This is not a very exciting amount, especially considering you have to invest more than $20,000 to achieve it.

But what if I told you that you could achieve those $900 by only investing $200, yes, you heard me—$200! This is not a printing error!

The investment world is wonderful. There are tools of leverage that allow one to obtain these returns in a short period of time, using only that which I have shared with you.

11

LEVERAGE

U p until now, we have used technical and fundamental analyses to make investment decisions. We know when to buy and sell, and now we must discover which instruments or ways of investing are the most profitable.

Traditionally, in the financial sector, some institutions have something called "margin accounts." These accounts allow you to buy double, triple, and in some cases, up to 20 times the capital that you have in your account. For example, if in your broker account you have $5,000, they allow you buy up to $20,000 by using leverage. Out of this amount, $5,000 are yours and they would be your maximum risk, while $15,000 are theirs.

The advantage of this type of account is that you can make more money, but it has a strong disadvantage because all of the money in your account is **AT RISK.** In other words, if you make an investment and it does not work, your account can end up in zero easily.

It is for this reason that I have specialized in learning about the financial derivatives market, or "options", more specifically. This tool allows leverage of 100 times more, meaning that you can achieve the desired goal by investing 100 times less and limiting your losses to the amount invested.

For example, if I have an account of $5,000 and purchase a financial option that costs $200, my maximum risk is only $200. The $4,800 cash in the account would not be affected by this operation.

Purchasing an option is like buying 100 ETFs for a specific period of time, and only paying a small fraction of money since it is for a limited amount of time

Options are financial contracts that give us the right to buy or sell an asset such as SPY at a determined price during a specified period of time. It is like buying insurance which you must pay a fee for.

Financial options have a price that is independent to the stock or ETF. Options have supply and demand but their prices are correlated with the type of options mentioned below.

There are only two types of options: **CALL** and **PUT**.

CALL options are used when we think that the price of something will go up. **PUT** options are used if we think that prices will fall. Obviously, both of these are used with the goal of making money.

Both of these options are very similar to "forwards" and "futures." It is like agreeing on a price for something to be able to buy or sell at that price in the future.

As you can imagine, we have worked with the S&P 500 because we are going to use financial options of the S&P 500 to make money. You now know that you must consult with the graph before making any purchasing decision. Now, let's take a look at what you should buy when that happens.

Let's take a look at which components have options:

1. There are two types of financial options: **CALL** and **PUT**. CALLS are used in upward trends as is the case of SPY, and PUTS are used in downward trends as is the case of SPDR Gold Trust and iShares Silver Trust (GLD and SLV). We must always keep in mind that what works best in upward trends are CALLS, and if we believe something will go up and want to make money, we must look at CALL contracts.

2. Financial options have an expiration date, meaning that if the movement you invested in and thought would take place does not occur by the date, they will expire and the value of the option will become zero.

3. They have a "strike price." This is the price at which we have the right to buy or sell a stock or ETF. For example, if you bought a strike at $202 with SPY and the price rises to $211, as it happened in the last example, you would earn $9 per contract, which multiplied by 100, would yield $900. Depending on time, your option might have cost something between $100 and $200. That is to say, there was a profit of $700. Interestingly, this was achieved with $200 and most likely in a period of two to three weeks.

4. Options are a **financial derivative**, meaning they are derived from something first. In this case, for SPY options to exist, SPY needs to exist first. If we are going to buy Apple options, it is because Apple exists. Options react to the movements of the active (ETF or stocks). For example, if Apple rises by 4% in one day, CALL options of Apple can increase by 100% or more. This is what makes options much more interesting, because they react or move faster than stocks and ETFs, given that they are leveraged.

5. Options have a separate independent price to that of the active price, i.e., they are correlated with SPY or with any stock, but the price of the options varies depending on other factors such as the "strike price", volatility, and time among others. For example, renting something for a month is not the same as renting something for a year, meaning that the further the expiration date is, the higher the fee that the investor will have to pay is. In the case of the "strike price", the further away the strike is from the spot price, the more expensive it will be, and vice versa.

6. Options also have a daily volume of transactions made, similar to stocks, but this volume tends to be much lower than that of the stock market.

Applied Example:

1. **Will the asset increase or decrease?**

   What we have discussed is that when SPY touches the moving average of 100 and breaks the channel in an "hourly" time frame it tends to rise, for which we must look for CALL options.

2. **What strike price should I choose?**

   What I normally use are two dollars above the spot price, meaning that if the price of SPY at the time is 202, I would choose strikes 204 or 205, maximum. The prices the stock has not reached yet are called "out of the money." These prices are more economical and more sensitive to price changes in the stock.

3. **For how long is it going to increase?**

   For this, we need to review the history. Normally SPY rises between $6 to approximately $10, and does so in a period between 2 to 4 weeks. This would be the expiration date we choose.

4. **What actives should I buy options from?**

   Through experience, I have come to the conclusion that the smartest thing to do is to invest in S&P 500. SPY is the best choice is because:

- It is the financial active of the greatest volume.
- The graph is predictable.
- It is volatile.
- It is important to focus on a single active. In this case, the largest in the world (SPY).

By answering these questions, we have all the elements to buy our financial option:

Active: (SPY).

Expiration date: 3 weeks more than the actual date.

Strike price: The spot price is, for example, $202 + $2 = strike price of $204.

Fee: It can be between $100 and $200 max (which would be the value at risk and this would be the value that increases as the price of SPY goes up).

5. **Calculating approximate profit:** If the price of SPY goes up to $212, our profit would be: Final price $212 – strike price $204 = 8 × 100 = $800

To this, we subtract the amount invested. In our example, we put in between $100 and $200, meaning that the profit generated was between $600 and $700 per contract. This translates to 600% or 700% profit in only three weeks. This profit is not calculated in annual cash terms. In that case, it would be with many more zeroes added to the right.

These profits are very important. In my experience as an investor, I have never seen anything like it. This is one of the smartest and fastest avenues you can take to generate earnings in the stock market.

Financial options are part of an exciting world and I would like to invite you to read more about this topic on our website **uoptions.com** and participate in our events. What you have just learned is just the beginning of a limitless world in which different rules apply and for which there are different responsibilities. Move forward and do not stop. With these tools that I am giving you, no one will be able to stop you!

How about this example of profit?

- Weekly options: Visit **uptions.co** to learn this strategy.

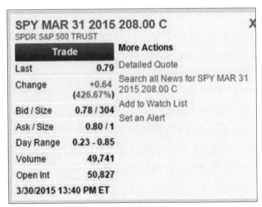

Source: Scottrade.com - SPY MAR 31

This means that in one day, this financial option rose 426%! Now I want to show you some examples of the profit that can be achieved using financial options.

CHART 6

Brokerage Balances	
Settled Funds Available for Trading:	$902.;
Funds Available for Trading:	$902.;
Total Cash Balance:	$902.;
Total Brokerage Account Value:	$8,339.;

View: 6 months ▼

Balance Deta

☒ Chart is current as of previous day's close.

Orders Edit ▲ ☐

Open: Sort By: Order Time ▼	Completed: Sort By: Execution Time ▼
You have no open orders.	You have no recently completed orders.

Positions Edit ▲ ☐

Symbol ▲	Qty	Last Price	Chg $|%	Mkt Value	Total Chg $	Total G/L $	Volur
AXP MAR 20 2015 85.00 C	4	2.53	+24.02%	1,012.00	+196.00	+320.00	2
CME MAR 20 2015 90.00 C	3	5.20	+71.05%	1,560.00	+648.00	+895.26	

Source: Scottrade.com

These are the options of American Express and the CME Group. Their profits are found in 'Total Gain and Loss." In the first case, you can have a profit of $230, and in the second case, you can have $895.26 from a jump in one of these financial actives.

In the "Symbol" section, we can first see the name of the stock, then we can see the expiration date, followed by the strike price (the price we believe the stock will reach and pass through). Then we see a "C," which means CALL. The "last price" tells us the price the option is currently at, and lastly, we can see that the volume of this option traded that day.

CHART 7

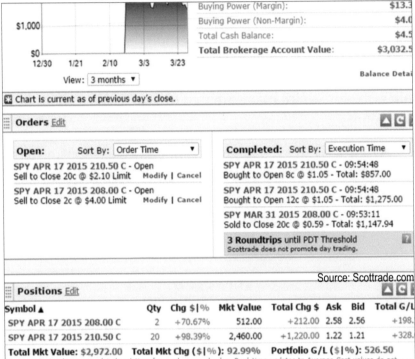

Source: Scottrade.com

In this table, we have SPY options. As we can see, in only one day, it had profits of 70.67% and 98.39%. The active is SPY, the expiration date is April 17, the strike price in the first case is $208, and in the second case it is $210.50. They are both CALL options.

Then we see "Qty" or contract quantity (2 and 20 respectively) change throughout the day in % and actual value, as well as the BID (price at which investors would pay if I wanted to sell) and ASK (price I would have to pay if I wanted to buy more). Remember that you are always going to buy cheap to sell expensive. If you see a big gap between the BID and ASK values, I do not recommend buying that active, which is why I always prefer SPY.

Finally, we can see the profits in the "Total G/L" box, which in this case, was $526.50. You should note that this happened in only one day. In many cases, I have seen profits in options reach 2,000% and 3,000% in very short periods of time. If you want to learn more about this topic, visit our website **uoptions. co** and observe how we make money, live. You can also attend our seminars, which many are free to you. I hope to hear from you soon!

I would like to show you how the option chains look, i.e., the dates, available strikes, and some other terms that you should know, as well as the variations that take place before the stock, as is the case of SPY.

CHART 8

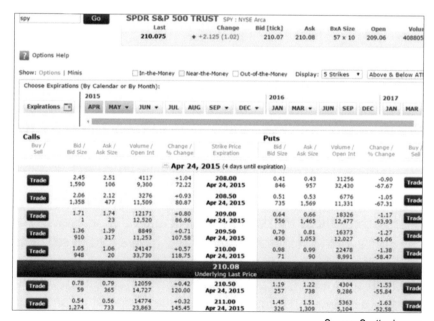

Source: Scottrade.com

In **CHART 8,** we can observe the following: the active that we see is S&P 500 (SPY), which had a variation of 1.02%, corresponding to $2.12.

Then we see three boxes: **In the money, Near the money,** and **Out of the money.**

Let's clarify **In the money** first: If the current price of SPY is $210.07 per stock, then all the strike prices that are lower than its price are defined as **In the Money**, because SPY has already passed or surpassed these price levels. This means strikes 208 and 210 are **In the Money.**

Normally, those prices are a little more expensive because they have an intrinsic value. Remember that financial options are a right to buy (in the case of CALLS) and to sell (in the case of PUTS). If I buy strike 208, when the spot price of SPY is $210, there is already an intrinsic value of $2 attached to it. If the reader checks the price of that strike, they will realize that the ASK is $2.51, meaning that the option costs $251, the intrinsic value is $200, and the $51 is the value of time being bought. In this case, it is one week.

The purple line in the graph indicates the spot price for SPY or whichever active is being studied. In this case, the price is $210.08, and then we see strikes that are **Out of the Money** ($210.5 and $211).

To find CALLS, we must look at the left side of the box. We see that the BID and ASK in the $211 strike are 0.54 Bid and 0.56 Ask. This means that if I were to buy, they would sell them to me for $0.56 each one and if I were to sell them, they would be bought for $0.54.

At the top, you can see different dates to choose from and the more time you buy, the more you will have to pay for the purchase.

The options that have the most amount of volume (transactions that have taken place) are seen to have the shortest amount of time bought; one or two weeks. And in the strikes found **Out of the Money,** they are generally 2 or 3 dollars above the spot price.

The reason I use these strikes and periods of time of one or two weeks is because I can invest little money and achieve profits of up to 500%, or in many cases, much more than that, in just one day. Remember to visit our website at **uoptions.com** where you can see how to make successful investments step by step.

CHART 9

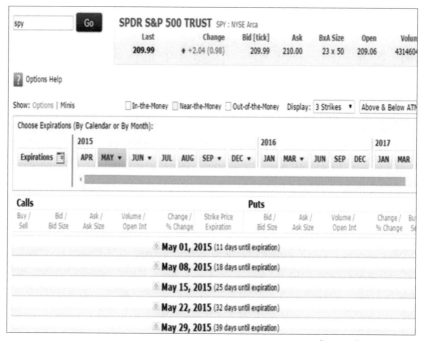

Source: Scottrade.com

To conclude, you should always remember that options have an expiration date: every Friday of every week.

For example, the week of May 01, 2015, expires on Friday that week. If I buy May 8, I have time to sell until the end of day. However, If I buy my option on May 4 and on that same day, I doubled my money, I do not have to wait until it expires. Instead, I can sell it on the same day since I achieved my profit goal. **The expiration date only tells me the date limit for me to sell, but in reality, I can sell at any given time before the deadline.**

In **CHART 8**, we can see that the strikes 210, 210.5, and 211 had a big increase of 100% in one day, meaning that your value doubled due to the rise in SPY. The variation can be seen in the "CALLS %" section on each of the strikes. As you can see, you are entering the right business, since these profits are hardly achieved with any other instrument in the world.

Here are a few basic rules to take into account:

1. **Do NOT invest** any amount that you are not willing to risk.

2. **Never use the capital of other people** for investments.

3. **Before** investing, run simulations for at least one month (Paper money).

4. **Remember:** the best investment is learning how to invest.

5. **Never give money to anyone.** Your task is to learn how to invest yourself.

6. **Opportunities repeat themselves,** so do not risk more than 10% of the account on each trade.

7. **Control your risks and use the graphs** to make decisions.

8. **Learn how to buy but also sell:** do not let greed take away your profits.

9. **Learn how to take your profits on time:** if you don't, the market may take them from you.

10. **Only focus on the S&P 500:** This will make you an expert in a single active so you will not need to waste time or be distracted by other stocks or indexes.

11. **In this business, as is in many sports, it is very important to have a guide or coach.** Learn with us. We have hundreds of students that have become successful with our strategies and methods.

As a Bonus, I want to give you 5 powerful strategies with which you can buy CALLS and make a profit during upward trends:

1. In the time frame of "**daily**", prices must touch a hard floor (price levels visited twice or three times in a period of 1 or 2 years). Then, in the timeframe of "**hourly**", I must draw a downward line and when prices break that line, they indicate an important probability of a future increase in prices.

2. For this strategy, we have to be in an upward trend in "**hourly**". Additionally, a fall must take place and prices must be close to the moving average of 40. Then I will trace a downward line and when it breaks said line, it indicates that I should buy CALL options.

3. The third strategy is when prices break or rupture the roof of a downward channel in an "hourly" time frame. This signifies future price increases.

4. When prices break the floor of a channel and return after hours or even days to the same level, this gives a signal that the ascending patterns from earlier will continue from then on, as the market moves in cycles. It can also be seen as re-entering the channel.

5. In this strategy, we must first see a hard drop (5, 6 or more points in SPY). I will keep extending the traced line on the upper part, and when it breaks the roof, this is a confirmation to buy CALL options.

The following graph describes **STRATEGY 1:**

STRATEGY 1 | PART A

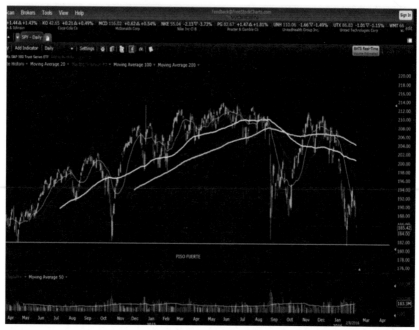

Source: freestockcharts.com

The following graph indicates that we must switch to an "hourly" time frame to make the decision to buy:

STRATEGY 1 | PART B

Source: freestockcharts.com

STRATEGY 2

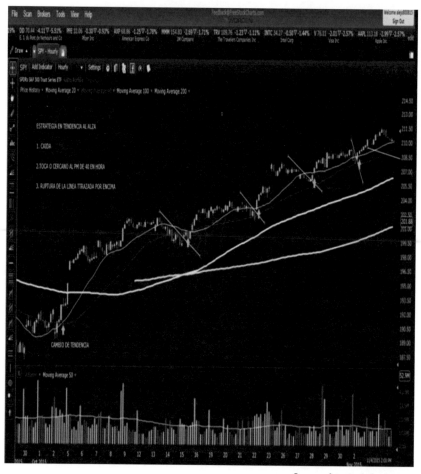

Source: freestockcharts.com

STRATEGY 3

Source: freestockcharts.com

STRATEGY 4

Source: freestockcharts.com

First, prices exited the channel that they were in for over a year. Then, as it re-entered the channel, you can see that it rose to levels close to what it had reached in the past.

STRATEGY 5

Source: freestockcharts.com

This strategy presents itself on several occasions, and it contains the ideal scenario to buy a CALL option:

- **Hard drop:** Remember that falls are opportunities.

- **"Hammers"** as signal that the fall is stopping.

- **Rupture of downward channel,** which is a factor in each strategy and it gives me the exact time, in "hourly", to make my purchase.

I hope you enjoyed this Bonus at the end of the book. Now it is time to take action! Sign-up to one of our seminars and start to make money with the stock market!

GLOSSARY

ACTIVE. Represents the property and rights of the company. Within the concept of goods are the cash, inventories, fixed assets, etc. The concept of rights may classify accounts receivable, investments in role of the market, valuations, etc.

ADMINISTRATOR OF THE ISSUE. Financial intermediary that is responsible for the processes related with the issue, placement and redemption of emissions of securities.

ADR. American Depositary Receipts. Negotiable certificates that are listed on one or more stock markets, different from the market of origin of the emission and constitute the property of a certain number of shares. They were created by Morgan Bank in 1927 in order to encourage the placement of foreign securities in the United States. When the negotiation is to be performed in that country the American Depositary Receipts ADR is constituted and pretend transactions outside the United States are made, programs such as the Global Depositary Receipts – GDR are established.

FINANCIAL ANALYSIS. A set of principles, techniques and procedures that are used to transform the information reflected on financial statements, in processed information usable for the economic decision-making, such as new investments, mergers of companies, granting of credit, etc.

FUNDAMENTAL ANALYSIS OR STRUCTURAL. Focused analysis of the stock market, which is studying all the relevant factors that may influence the future behavior of profits and dividends of companies and therefore the price of their shares. Under this theory the determining factor is the "value of the company and the price of the action will always be set to this value.

TECHNICAL ANALYSIS. Focused analysis of the stock market, which is studying all the factors related with the history, the price and the volume of the action, mainly through the use of graphs with the purpose to predict future changes in the trend of that asset.

BALANCE SHEET. The situation accounting demonstrative economic finances of a firm in a given period of time.

EXCHANGE BALANCE. Descriptive instrument in the short term of the external sector. Can be defined as the recording of transactions of a particular Central bank with assets of international reserves, other liabilities and external assets of short and medium term. Since these values are the availability of liquidity in foreign currency of the central bank, one can also say that the exchange balance is the cash accounting in foreign currency of that institution.

TRADE BALANCE. Difference between exports and imports of goods from one country, does not include international trade in services. If exports are greater than imports, there is a trade surplus and if imports are higher than exports, there is a trade deficit.

BALANCE OF PAYMENTS. Account for the external sector of the System of National Accounts, expressed in dollars, where are recorded economic transactions of a country with the outside. Among these are the buying and selling of goods, capital movements and transfers. In addition, summarizes the changes in the financial position of the residents of a country compared to non-residents. The balance of payments is composed of the current account, by the capital account, the movement in international reserves and a line where errors are logged and omissions.

BALANCE OF SERVICES. Systematic registration of the entry and exit of foreign currency of a country by way of provision of services of the residents of the country to foreigners and to nationals. The balance of services is part of the current account and it included as services net revenues precedents of the outside (shipments, travel, dividends and interest from direct or portfolio investment among others).

COMMERCIAL BANKING. Set of private financial institutions that have as their main function the receipt of deposits and the disbursement of short-term loans.

DEVELOPMENT BANK. Financial institutions responsible for providing technical advice on projects and to support specific sectors of productive activity by lending operations or invest-ment, generally at lower interest rates than those offered in the market.

INVESTMENT BANKING. Activity developed by an intermediary of the financial market which may include the diagnosis of companies, the organization of potential buyers, the advice of investors in the creation of new enterprises and even the achievement of resources for such operations.

FOREIGN BANKING. Branches of foreign banks that carry out their activities from the commercial banks.

THE CENTRAL BANK. Is the entity responsible for the conduct of the monetary policy of a country? In exercise of this function the Central Bank generally has the monopoly on issuing legal currency, therefore, the central bank, depending on the economic conditions of the country (inflation, unemployment, etc.), decides to issue more tickets or, on the contrary, collect part of all those who are in circulation. The Central Bank has two primary functions, on the one hand must preserve the value of the currency and to maintain price stability and on the other, ensure the functioning and maintain the stability of the payment system in an economy because the central bank is the bank of banks, their clients are not ordinary people or individual companies, but the State and the banks existing within the territory of the nation to which it belongs.

COMMERCIAL BANK. Institution that is devoted to the business of receiving money on deposit and give it to your time on loan, either in the form of mutual, of discount of documents or in any other way. Are also viewed as all operations which naturally and legally constitute the Giro. Second-floor bank. Financial institutions that do not deal directly with the users of the credits but that make the exposures of the same through other financial institutions.

MORTGAGE BANK. These institutions are distinguished from the trade by requiring root property as a guarantee of the credits.

BOLLINGER BANDS. Tool used to make technical analysis of a financial asset. Allows one to obtain support and resistance levels on short-term dynamics which are calculated on the basis of an average exponential on prices (income), to which are added two bands obtained applying two standard deviations to the result of that average above and below. Reflect the volatility of prices (or income) during a period. The higher the volatility that is present in the market, the greater the standard deviation and therefore the bands will be more extensive, and vice versa. When the width of the band is less than what is observed is historically signal that is approaching an important movement in the prices (or income).

MONETARY BASE. Monetary aggregate that can be interpreted as a set of monetary obligations acquired by the Central Bank with the general public and the financial system.

BEAR MARKET. Shows a trend calm in the capital market, usually when investors are to the expectation of some macroeconomic information and therefore denotes a declining market. See: Bull Market.

BEIGE BOOK. It is a report in which each Bank, member of the United States Federal Reserve, provides information with regard to the economic conditions of each district based on interviews with bankers and entrepreneurs as well as interviews with economists, market specialists and other sources. Published eight times a year and its impact on the market is important due to the depth of its analysis.

BENCHMARK. Standard point of reference against which comparisons are performed.

BENEFICIARY. Person to which a financial asset is being transferred to or to whom is issued a title or an insurance contract.

PRIMARY BENEFICIARY. Is the person who acquires a new title value before the CA, either through the securities market or its delegate to this effect.

DURABLE GOOD. Well that is not consumed immediately and that lasts a long time providing successively and many times, the service for which it was created.

CAPITAL GOODS. Are those assets that are used for the production of other and do not meet the needs of the final summing. These include the machinery and equipment.

CONSUMER GOODS. Goods intended to meet the needs of the final consumer home and that they are fit to be used or consumed without any additional commercial development.

INTERMEDIATE GOODS. Correspond to capital goods and are so called by the fact, to serve consumers in an indirect way to the satisfaction of their needs as they represent intermediate stages in the production process. Also known as raw materials or inputs.

NON-TRADABLE GOODS. Goods whose consumption can only be done within the economy in which they produce cannot be imported or exported. This is due to the fact that these products have very high transport costs or exists in the economy a high degree of protectionism.

TRADABLE GOODS. Those goods that can be consumed within the economy that produces them and you can export and import. They generally have low transportation costs, few tariffs and import quotas that can block the free flow of goods across national borders.

BLUE CHIPS. Stocks that present great dividends, great valuation and excellent level of liquidity. They correspond to the best companies of a country, recognized by the quality of their products and financial statements.

BONDS. Are titles that represent a part of a credit constituted by a certification authority. Its minimum period is one year, in return for its investment will receive a fixed interest rate that the issuer in accordance with market conditions at the time of placing the placement of the titles. By its characteristics these titles are considered fixed-income. In addition to the ordinary bonds, exist in the market bonds of garment and warranty bonds general, specific and bonds convertible into shares.

AMORTISING BOND. Is one bonus that mitigates the principal before maturity and interest payments during his life.

BRADY BONDS. Titles of sovereign debt issued by certain developing countries, in exchange for the restructuring of its commercial debt and other previous obligations. Are bonds of public issue denominated in dollars, created to restructure the debt of some emerging market governments declared in moratorium at the beginning of the eighties. Between the issuing countries are Argentina, Brazil, Mexico, Nigeria, among others. Colombia does not have this type of bond due to that never defaulted on its payments.

BONUS BULLET. Is one Bonus that pays 100% of the nominal value at maturity.

BONUS CALLABLE. Is one bonus that includes a call option, which gives the right to the issuer to redeem the voucher before their expiry date of agreement to certain conditions. Zero coupon bond. Is that bond that has no coupon payments newspapers, but that in consideration is sold at a discount to their nominal value.

GLOBAL BOND. Are hybrid bonds, i.e. are designed to be traded, positioned and met simultaneously in the Eurobond market and in USA.

BOND PUTTABLE. Is one bonus that includes a put option, which gives the investor the ability to sell the bond the issuer to the par value on a particular date.

CONVERTIBLE BONDS IN STOCKS (PORTS). This class of titles confer the prerogatives of the ordinary bonds and in addition give their holders the right or the option to convert them in whole or in part in shares of the respective issuing company.

GENERAL WARRANTY BONDS. Those who are issued by financial corporations.

TREASURY BONDS. Expression generally used to refer to an obligation of the Treasury of the United States, negotiable and issued to different deadlines. According to maturity take different names: Treasury bills, zero-coupon securities with a maturity of less than one year, Treasury notes, titles with coupon and maturities between one and ten years, Treasury bonds, titles and zero coupon maturing between ten and thirty years.

ORDINARY BONDS. Are those which give their holders the same rights, in accordance with the respective broadcasting contract and are guaranteed with all the goods of the broadcaster are present or future.

SAMURAI BONDS. Bonds issued in Japan by non- Japanese residents in yen.

SOVEREIGN BONDS. Generic term used for bonds issued by the government of any country.

BONDS OF GARMENT. Value title issued by a general store of deposit, which incorporates an inventory credit on the goods covered by the certificate of deposit and confers, by itself, the rights and privileges of the garment.

BOVESPA. It is the Brazilian Stock Market, located in the largest city of the country, Sao Paulo, from where it derives its name. Under this acronym also appointed representative index of the evolution of the price of the shares transacted in this bag Bovespa Index. It is the largest stock values of Latin America. It is currently the bag for the negotiation of stock and their derivatives that more grows in America and the third largest in the world, in terms of volume means negotiated in dollars. Bovespa is linked to all the Brazilian exchanges, including the Rio de Janeiro, where they exchange the values of the government.

BROKER. Is the person or entity that acts as an intermediary between a buyer and a seller in securities transactions, charging a commission. The Broker acts as an agent, i.e. takes no position of its own even with temporary duration, if they are not limited to join two positions (sale) at a price that is satisfactory to both parties.

BROKERAGE. Action of intermediation where a broker or broker puts in contact to two natural persons or legal entities for the negotiation of a title value, without coming to intervene in the negotiation process.

BULL MARKET. Indicates an upward trend in the capital market, where investors are optimistic and therefore pressed quickly prices upward. See: Bear Market.

CAPITAL. The sum of all resources, goods and values mobilized for the constitution and commissioning of a company. Is your economic reason. Amount invested in a company by the owners, partners or shareholders.

PAID-IN CAPITAL. The part of the subscribed capital that the shareholders of the company have been fully paid, therefore has entered into the coffers of the company.

SOCIAL CAPITAL. Represents the collection of money, goods and services provided by the partners and constitutes the equity base of a company. This capital can be reduced or increased by new contributions, capitalization of reserve, enhancement of the heritage or the conversion of bonds into shares.

SUBSCRIBED CAPITAL. It is the part of the social capital authorized by subscribers of shares that have been obliged to pay in a given time.

CAPITALIZATION. Reinvestment or reapply the results, utilities or reservations, to the assets of the undertaking. Expansion of the capital paid through new issues of shares.

STOCK MARKET CAPITALIZATION. The value given to a company on the Stock Exchange. It is calculated by multiplying the price by the number of shares that make up the capital of that company. The capitalization of the values quoted on the stock market is the one that is obtained by adding all the contributions of those values in a given time. This index is used to compare stock markets.

CAPM (CAPITAL ASSET PRICING MODEL). Model that seeks to project the fair price of an asset, taking into account the expected return to that investment in particular and its level of risk.

CDAT (CERTIFICATE OF DEPOSIT SAVINGS TO TERM). As its name indicates is term savings, with a term of not less than five days and whose interests may be agreed freely with the customer. Are personal and cannot be negotiated in a secondary market. Do not constitute securities.

CDS (COLLATERALIZED DEBT OBLIGATIONS). A structured credit product. It is composed of assets that have different risk ratings, which can go from AAA titles to stock. It is an important vehicle for portfolio investment and diversification of risk.

CDS OR CREDIT DEFAULT SWAPS. Credit derivative contracts that allow the holder to protect themselves from the risk of default by the issuer.

CDS SPREAD. Annual amount to be paid by the buyer of a CDS to the seller during the term of the contract. It is expressed as a percentage of the nominal value.

CLEARING AND SETTLEMENT. Stock exchanges have a camera of clearing and settlement, which is responsible for registering, settle and compensate for operations of spot or forward made in bags by the agents. The functions of liquidating the cash transactions or to term, receive, deliver the values and monies corresponding to the operations carried out and advancing the procedures necessary to meet the transfer of the registered securities traded, are an efficient tool with which to count the bags for the safe implementation of the operations.

COMMISSION. Remuneration which gives an investor to a contractor to perform an order of purchase or sale of securities on the Stock Exchange, by assisting in the same or to manage the client values, depending on the request of the same.

CONTRACTOR OF BAG. The person legally authorized to perform the transactions of purchase and sale of securities that are performed on the wheel of the bag. Must be registered in the National Registry

COMMODITIES. Primary goods that are traded internationally. For example: grains, metals, energy products (oil, coal, etc.) and soft (coffee, cotton, etc.).

PRIVATE CONSUMPTION. What made the private entities in an economy (includes the companies) and is also known as personal consumption.

PUBLIC CONSUMPTION. Expenditure made by the State in goods and services. A high level of public consumption in relation to the private consumption indicates a high state intervention in the economy.

CORRELATION. Indicates the strength and direction of a linear relationship between two random variables. It is considered that two quantitative variables are correlated when the values of one of them vary systematically with respect to the values homonyms of the other: if we have two variables (A and B) correlation exists if the increase the values of to do so also for B and vice versa. The correlation between two variables does not by itself imply a causal relationship.

COVARIANCE. Represents the average of the product of the deviations of two variables in relation to its average. Statistical measure whose value represents a linear association between two variables. If the two variables are always simultaneously above or below the average covariance is positive, otherwise is negative. A value close to zero suggests little relation between the co-movements of the variables.

CREDIT QUALITY. Degree of compliance that the issuer has with regard to the obligations assumed with the issuance of the qualification. Object Risk rating in the short term. Analysis that aims to assess in the short term, the capacity of a specialized establishment in a commercial or industrial activity defined (sale of food, clothing, vehicles, etc.) to serve adequately for their credits.

CUSTOMS. Government service responsible for the valuation and collection of duties and taxes on imports and exports and the implementation of other laws and regulations that apply to the import, transit and export of articles.

DEMAND. Set of goods and services that consumers are willing to acquire in the market, in a particular time and at a given price. The analysis of the demand part of the assumption that all factors remain constant except the price, and that as it changes, the amount demanded by the consumer also varies.

DEPRECIATION. Gradual cuts in the debt through periodic payments on the borrowed capital. Recovery of funds invested in the assets of a company.

DERIVATIVES. Contracts referenced to an asset or an economic variable to be liquidated at a future date, on the basis of which it handled the risks of an investment portfolio. Are values whose price depends on the value of one or more variables, making it possible to isolate or concentrate an existing risk and transfer it to the market.

DERIVED NON-DELIVERY. It is an operation with derived constituted by sales under which a part sold to another about fixed-income securities, with the commitment to the latter to sell the first, at a later date and at the price established at the start of the operation, diplomas equivalent to those originally delivered.

DIVIDEND. In the event of having utilities in a company are the part that corresponds to the shareholder of the same. In other words, is the value paid to investors as a reward for its investment, either in cash or shares.

EBITDA. The acronym means in English Earnings Before Interest, Taxes, Depreciation and Amortization; is derived from the State of results and represents the margin or a gross operating profit of the company before the deduction of any interest, amortization or depreciation and Income Tax.

ETF. Investment funds are quoted on the stock exchange, being able to buy and sell over the course of a session to the existing price in each time without the need to wait for the closure of the market. They are known by its initials in English ETF (Exchange Trade Funds). Its aim is to replicate a stock exchange index or replicate a basket of financial assets.

EXERCISE OF THE OPTION. Moment in which the buyer or holder of a call option to purchase or sale put makes use of its right to buy or sell the underlying. In the event that the purchaser of the option decides to exercise it and the parties agree to its liquidation through the mechanism of compensation, it will receive from the seller of the option the difference in dollars between the index and the strike price.

BASIC FINANCIAL STATEMENTS. General Balance Sheet, Statement of Results, Statement of Changes in Equity, the statement of changes in financial position and Statement of Cash Flows.

CONSOLIDATED FINANCIAL STATEMENTS. Those that present the financial position, results of operations, changes in the heritage and the financial situation, as well as the cash flows of an entity array and its subordinates, a dominant entity and the dominated, as if they were those of a single company.

FLUCTUATION. Rise and fall of the changes in the values, currencies, etc., as a result of the effects of the supply and demand. Action of vary, modify, alter the value of the currency when it refers to the monetary change, economic phenomenon that brings the raises or lowers the representative prices in the book values.

FORWARDS. Private contract that represents the obligation to buy (or sell), a particular asset at a specified future date, in a preset price at the beginning of the period of validity of the contract.

FORWARD RATE AGREEMENT (FRA). Future agreement of interest rate that allows movements do not cover you want in the interest rates of a currency. This is to agree an interest rate for a specific period of time, which is counted from a date specified in the agreement and for a given nominal value.

HEDGE FUNDS. Investment fund or specialized coverage in the investments of speculative so that a natural or legal person to protect against changes in the prices of goods or shares.

FUTURES. That transaction is carried out in a formal secondary market, where is negotiated a contract standardized for the purchase or sale of a given asset, remembering the amount of the asset, its price and the expiration of the contract, assuming the parties the obligation to celebrate and the commitment to pay or receive the losses or gains produced by the differences of the contract price, during the term of the same and its liquidation.

GDR (GLOBAL DEPOSIT RECEIPTS). Certificates that can move freely in the global capital markets that denote stocks of foreign companies; these certificates are registered in Luxembourg. Are the equivalent global (European) for the ADR. Underlying these certificates have the property of some stock in some foreign market. In reality they are not so common nor its market is so liquid as the ADR.

GUARANTEE. Figure by which an entity undertakes to respond by certain obligations acquired by another entity, in the event that the latter, as the main obliged, the breach. In the case of emissions in the securities market The guarantee you must grant a credit establishment guarded by the Banking Superintendence.

IDB (INTER-AMERICAN DEVELOPMENT BANK). Its goal is to finance development projects and mutual assistance in the nations of the American continent, in addition to promoting the economic growth and social development of member countries.

IDB-TO-COVER. In an auction, refers to the relationship between the bids submitted and the amount offered.

CAPITAL INCREASE. Incorporation into the capital of the company of reservations and/or new resources, carried out normally by subscription rights to the shareholders. Requires the approval of the Assembly of shareholders or the directory in case of authorized capital.

INDEX. Indicator that is intended to measure the variations of an economic phenomenon or of another order referred to a value that is taken as a basis in a given time. Stock market indices. A stock index corresponds to a composite statistical, usually a number, which seeks to reflect variations in the value or profitability average of shares of which it is composed. Generally, the stock that make up the index have common characteristics such as: belonging to one and the same stock exchange, have a similar market capitalization or belonging to a same industry. These are usually used as a point of reference for different portfolios such as mutual funds.

BETA INDICATOR. Indicator of systemic risk or the market for investment in shares, which allows you to set how sensitive is the behavior of the profitability of an action when there are movements in the profitability of the stock market. If the value of BETA for an action is equal to 1, means that the yields of this vary so pro-Proportional to market yields, i.e. that the stock have the same performance as the market. On the other hand, a BETA greater than 1 means that the performance of the action varies in a more than proportional to the performance of the market. And a beta less than 1 means that the action varies in a less than proportional to the market.

INTERMEDIATION IN THE SECURITIES MARKET. Refers to the completion of operations that have the purpose or effect the rapprochement of plaintiffs and bidders for the acquisition or disposal of values inscribed in the National Registry of Securities and intermediaries, is that these operations are performed by their own account or for hire or reward, on the stock market or in the market tour, primary or secondary.

FINANCIAL LEVERAGE. Indebtedness of a company with the aim of increasing their productive capacity and thus their sales.

LISTING. Price recorded in a bag when you perform a negotiation of values.

LONG-TERM INSTRUMENTS. The cast with amortization total to more than a year.

DERIVATIVE INSTRUMENTS. Are financial instruments, usually contracts that stipulate that the parties undertake to buy or sell, at a future date, a well determined that you can be a physical (commodities), currencies and financial instruments, to a value that is fixed at the time of negotiation.

M-1 (money supply). Corresponds to the means of payment or money supply and in practice is associated with what might be called money, collects the role of money as a means of payment; it is composed of the most liquid financial assets of the economy. The M1 includes cash in the hands of the public and in the financial system, the current account deposits, which are transferable by check. The subscript "1" suggests that there may be other definitions of money.

M-2 (monetary offer extended). Includes the payment means (M-1) plus the interest-bearing deposits, small term deposits, repurchase agreements from day to day.

M-3. Involves the M2 more the fiduciary deposits of the financial system, an item of liabilities of the financial entities called Other demand deposits, repos with the real sector and some accounts payable.

MARGIN OR SPREAD. Difference between the price of demand and supply in the quotation of an instrument, currency or title. Additionally, this term is used to indicate the difference in performance between two titles.

MARKET-MAKERS. Market makers are responsible for proclaiming permanently prices by those who are willing to buy or sell a certain amount of titles.

FUTURES MARKET. Where you buy and sell contracts of goods or values in which it makes use of a promise to some future date to pre-agreed prices in the negotiation. These future contracts, which make it possible to reduce the risk of fluctuations in prices in the short term, may be fixed or standardized by units of quantity, quality requirements, due date or other characteristics.

OPTIONS MARKET. Where rights are negotiated for the purchase or sale of a raw material or a financial product in a given period and at a fixed price.

OPTION. On the market in the long term, right to buy (call) or sell (put), at a scheduled time and at a fixed price, a raw material or a financial product. The right of the buyer of the option is exercised at its discretion, while for the sender is a contingent liability until the expiry of the option.

PRIMARY PLACEMENT. The supply of new titles by an entity to capture resources in order to develop their social object. Relationship between the acquirer or first beneficiary of the value.

PURCHASE OPTION (CALL). An operation with derived by virtue of which the party who acquires, gets the right to buy the underlying a date and a price determined and, in turn, the party that sells is obliged to sell such underlying. In the American options, the buyer of the option you can exercise at any time before and at the date of compliance.

OPTION OF SALE (PUT). An operation with derived by virtue of which the party who acquires, gets the right to sell the underlying a date and a price determined and, in turn, the party that sells is obliged to buy such underlying. In the American options, the seller of the option you can exercise at any time before and at the date of compliance.

QUALIFICATION OF VALUES. A professional opinion that produces a risk rating agency, on the ability of an issuer to repay the capital and interest of its obligations in a timely manner. To reach this opinion, rating agencies have developed studies, analyzes and evaluations of issuers. The qualification of values is the result of the need to give investors of new tools for the decision making.

COUPON RATE. Periodic interest rate that the issuer of a title promises to pay the holder until the expiration of the title. It is expressed as an annual percentage of the nominal value of the title.

INTERNAL RATE OF RETURN (IRR). Tool for the analysis of profitability of flows of funds, which is defined as the discount rate of the flows in which the net present value is equal to zero. Corresponds to the profitability that would get an investor to maintain the financial instrument until its extinction, under the assumption that reinvests the income flows at the same rate.

ROA (PROFITABILITY OF ACTIVE). Return on asset. Financial reason that shows the profitability of the company generated from its total assets. This is calculated as net profit on Total Assets.

ROE (PROFITABILITY OF HERITAGE). Return on equity. Financial reason that shows the profitability of the company generated from their heritage. This is calculated as net profit on total equity.

ROI (RETURN ON INVESTMENT). Relates the utilities with the performance obtained on the investment.

SALES IN SHORT. Corresponds to the disposal of an asset on which the seller is in a "short" position and are made exclusively on titles obtained previously in a temporary securities transfer operation. The sale of securities that at the time of the negotiations are not of your property. For the purposes of the operation of temporary transfer of values, you must purchase or reinstate the titles to the initial holder.

S&P 500 (STANDARD & POOR'S 500). It is one of the most important stock market indices in the United States. This index records the average behavior of all the stock market in the United States and is composed of the price of the 500 most important companies in that country.

SEC (SECURITY EXCHANGE COMMISSION). American independent agency, responsible for monitoring the stock market. Sailing by the respect for professional ethics and to the right of the shareholders. Is equivalent to the Securities Commission (COB) in France and to the Securities Superintendence in Colombia.

SHARE: Title of ownership of negotiability representative of an aliquot part of the heritage of a company or firm. Attaches to its holder's rights which may be exercised collectively and/or individually.

SHARES IN CIRCULATION. Number of shares issued by a company that can be freely transacted in the market.

SHARE OF ENJOYMENT. One that is delivered to a partner to offset contributions from service.

SHARE INACTIVE. One that has not registered the official listing on any stock exchange in the country during the last thirty (30) calendar days.

ORDINARY SHARE: Action that has the feature to grant the holder certain rights of participation in the issuing company among which is the to perceive dividends and the vote in the Assembly.

SHAREHOLDER. The person that owns shares and holder of the title that represents, who also has been duly registered in the register of shareholders of the respective issuing company.

SPLIT. Fragmentation of the shares resulting from a decrease in their nominal value and is proportional to the same. Is the division of the number of shares in circulation of a society in a greater number of shares; in such a way that each action in circulation gives you the right to its holder, receiving in exchange a certain number of new shares. The heritage of the shareholder remains stable because although he possesses more share, they lowered the price as the value of all the shares together remains the same, (at the end, the total value for the investor does not vary, only change the price and the amount of shares).

STATE OF CASH FLOW. Seeks to establish inflow and outflow of cash that have had or may have a company in the future. This statement is used to determine the status of the liquidity of the company, to determine the feasibility of projects or to measure profitability or future growth of a business.

STATE OF RESULTS. The state of results or losses or gains shows the income and expenditure as well as the profit or loss resulting from the operations of the company during a certain period of time, usually a year. It is a dynamic state, since it reflects an activity. Is cumulative, i.e. summarizes the operations of a company from the first to the last day of the period.

STOCK EXCHANGE. Private establishment authorized by the national Government where they meet the members that make up the bag in order to perform the operations of purchase – sale of securities, on account of its clients, especially. Public site where they perform the meetings of the bag or carry out the transactions of the same. The modern idea of "site", can be associated with "virtual place" where is the supply and demand of values.

SWAP. Private contracts between two entities to exchange cash flows in the future, according to preset conditions. Can be considered as forward contracts.

T-BONDS. Word which in Spanish means US Treasury Bonds. It is a debt instrument that has as due date a maximum of thirty years.

TITLES OF FIXED INCOME. Representative titles of a debt that gives to those who possesses them, the right to receive a fixed interest rate for a fixed period.

TITLES OF VARIABLE INCOME. Securities in which profitability is known only after redemption. Its performance depends on the economic performance of the company. In general terms corresponds to the shares issued by a corporation.

UNDERLYING. Active, rate or stock index of reference, whose price movement determines the cost in an operation with derivative or a spot operation, such as: exchange rate, interest rate, foreign exchange, commodities, stock indices, titles, etc.

VALUE IN BOOKS. Reference value of an action, which takes into consideration only the value of the company, understood as the value of its assets less its obligations on the total shares in circulation. In this sense the book value does not take into consideration the potential for the recovery of the company in the future, but only its current value.

INTRINSIC VALUE. In options, to calculate this value we must take the final price or spot and subtracting the strike price. (price at the end of the exercise - strike price= intrinsic value).

VALUE OF THE TITLE. The face value or the headings in a spot operation or in an operation with derivative whose underlying are titles.

VIX. Indicator of Risk aversion that indicates the expected volatility of stock index of United States S&P 500 for 30 days. It is expressed in percentage.

YEAR TO DATE. Term used to refer to the period from the first of January of the current year and the current day or the last day for which data are available for the variable for which you want to perform the calculation: an index, variation, figure or indicator. When you have a monthly or quarterly observation the term year shall cover the period between January or the first quarter of the current year according to the case and the current month or quarter. In English is known as YTD (Year to Date).

VIX. Indicador de aversión al riesgo que señala la volatilidad esperada del índice accionario de Estados Unidos S&P 500 para los 30 días siguientes. Se expresa en porcentaje.

For me it is an honor that you have read my book.

Thank you very much!

Hope this has helped in the process, keep learning and I assure you overcome any giant. I hope to meet you soon personally.

Blessings!

Made in the USA
Columbia, SC
18 December 2024

50075814R00082